OVER THE HORIZON

1939 - 1945

by

LIEUTENANT COMMANDER
ALAN J. M. MILLER DSC VRD
Clyde Division RNVR

Old men forget; yet all shall be forgot
But he'll remember, with advantages
What feats he did that day. Then shall our names
Familiar in his mouth as household words
Be in their flowing cups freshly remembered.

W.S. - KING HENRY V

Finavon Print & Design

First Published in Great Britain in 1999
by Finavon Print & Design, 3 Cadgers Path, Finavon, Angus. DD8 3QB

Copyright © Alan J.M. Miller

ISBN 0-9528813-6-5

Front cover: **HMS BROCKLESBY**, *Hunt Class Destroyer (L42) - the Author's ship from June 1941 - Novemebr 1942.*
Rear Cover: *The Author as Captain of* **HMS HOLDERNESS** *in 1945*

To Kirsteen

- without doubt

"Duty is the great business of a Sea - Officer" - Captain Nelson of HMS Boreas to his fiancée, Fanny Nisbet, on 4th May 1786

Kirsteen, Alan's wife, as a WAAF in 1940 aged 20

FOREWORD

In the wardroom of the cruiser in which I was serving in 1939, there was only one RNVR officer. In the wardroom of my destroyer in 1945, I was the only one who wasn't a Reserve officer.

It was they who manned the ships at sea and the establishments ashore as the Navy rapidly increased in size and competence to meet its manifold commitments throughout the world.

Alan Miller was one of that small band of RNVR officers who led this 'revolution' from the very first days of the war, and this remarkable tale of his adventures well illustrates the wide variety of duties they were called upon to undertake. It also provides an invaluable account of the actions and campaigns in which he took part, as well as a vivid description of how, as young men, we lived and fought through those eventful years.

I so well remember Alan's arrival aboard Brocklesby, newly commissioned in 1941, when we felt severely over-stretched and woefully short of experience. His enthusiasm and competence gave a much needed boosts to our endeavours, and it was with complete confidence and satisfaction that I handed over my First Lieutenant's duties to him some ten months later.

From then on Alan progressed rapidly up the ladder of responsibility and in less than two years achieved his first Command, to be followed by two more before the war's end. He came to know well the hardships and, all too often, the horrors of convoy escort duties in the face of relentless weather and determined enemy attack, across the wide expanse of the Atlantic, in the narrow seas of the Channel, and along the Arctic route to Murmansk.

Few can have had such a varied war, nor better served its cause. I am delighted that he has written these recollections and honoured to contribute this foreword to them.

Commander L E Peyton-Jones CVO DSO MBE DSC† RN, 14th November 1998

CONTENTS

List of Abbreviations

AMC	Armed Merchant Cruiser
AWOL	Absent Without Leave
CW	Commissioned Warrant
(D)	Destroyer
DCT	Direction Control Tower
DE	Destroyer Escort
DF	Destroyer Flotilla
D/F	Direction Finder (ing)
(E)	Engineer
FN	Forth-North convoy
FOIC	Flag Officer in Charge
FS	Forth-South convoy
(G)	Gunnery
HA/LA	High Angle/Low Angle anti-aircraft gun
HF/DF	High Frequency Direction Finding
HMT	His Majesty's Transportship
HNS	Homeward-bound convoy to UK
LCF	Landing Craft Flak
LCP	Landing Craft Personnel
LRE	Long Range Escort
LSI	Landing Ship Infantry
LST	Landing Ship Tank
MAEE	Marine Aircraft Experimental Establishment
MGB	Motor Gun Boat
ML	Minelayer
MTB	Motor Torpedo Boat
OKM	Oberkommando der Marine
ONS	Outward-bound convoy from UK
PPI	Plan Position Indicator radar
psc	passed staff course
PW	Portsmouth-West convoy
RN	Royal Navy
RNR	Royal Naval Reserve
RNVR	Royal Naval Volunteer Reserve
SBA	Sick Bay Attendant
SGB	Steam Gun Boat
SKL	Seekriegsleitung
SNO	Senior Naval Officer
SRE	Sound Reproduction Equipment
(T)	Torpedo
TBS	Talk between ships radio
VAD	Voluntary Aid Detachment
WP	West-Portsmouth convoy
WRNS	Womens' Royal Naval Service

Preface

Keeping a diary in wartime contravened King's Regulations and Admiralty Instructions for security reasons in the event of capture or salvage. However despite this stricture I have found my diaries invaluable enabling me to use an accurate timetable of events and a trigger for the recall of situations which may now be of interest, and a thread to guide the reader through six years of one man's war at sea.

Additionally when I realised I was going to range over the Seven Seas I bought a couple of maps of the world about 24" x 12" and drew a set of similar random co-ordinates on both: giving one to Kirsteen so when writing I could dot letters to indicate where in the world I was. Simple, secure and worked well through the years!

The title of this chronicle was inspired by a grandson's 'thank-you' letter following a cruise on *China Clipper* when I demonstrated that the world was round as islands hove out of the sea and he wrote "thank you for taking me over the horizon".

I am grateful to a number of old shipmates whose names appear in the text for their input to this book, but in particular I wish to thank my son Colonel A.K.M. Miller OBE for the skilful computer work and long hours he has invested in the project to the point where uniquely it was proof-read by the former Dean of the Faculty of Advocates, the Hon. Lord Kincraig and Anthony Murray of Dollerig. My thanks are also due to Commander W.M. Bisset the curator of the South African Naval Museum in Simon's Town for enthusiastic support.

HMS *Dorsetshire*, County Class Cruiser -
November 1939-May 1941

HMS *Orwell*, "O" Class Destroyer (G98)
- March 1943-February 1944

HMS *Brocklesby*, Hunt Class Destroyer (L42) -
June 1940-November 1942

HMS *Fitzroy*, Captain Class Frigate (K553) -
April-September 1944

HMS *Wolverine*, V&W Class Destroyer (I78) - March-June 1945

HMS *Holderness*, Hunt Class
Destroyer (L48) - July-September 1945

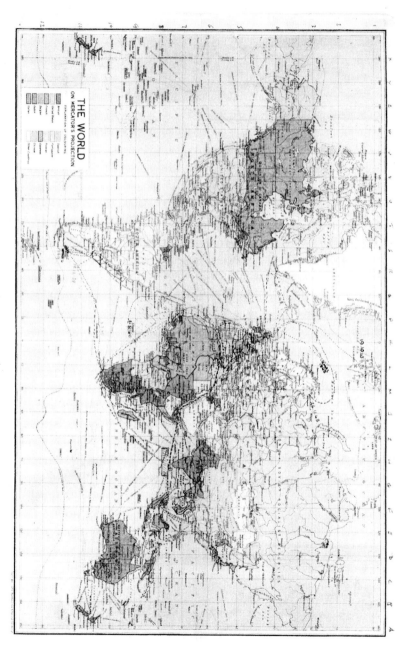

The World Map complete with the coded grid to allow Kirsteen to know the author's whereabouts on his travels throughout the war.

Chapter I

RNVR – PASSAGE EAST
23 August – November 1939

In the late nineteen-thirties the war clouds were gathering but at our age we didn't take it very seriously. In fact with the economy, particularly on Clydeside, booming on the back of a resurgence in shipbuilding and related manufacturing industries, there was a definite 'feel good' atmosphere around. Most of my friends in their teens had lived through the awful years of the 1930s depression and had felt, as I did, the desperation of the unemployed on the streets and at best the worries of our own parents in whatever business they were in. I will never forget in perhaps 1929 or 30 being taken during the school holidays by my father to visit a shipyard on Tyneside, where presumably he had an insulation contract or hopes of one, and driving through the streets of Newcastle and Sunderland with hundreds and hundreds of grey men standing around the streets with absolutely nothing to do. Clydeside was much the same and I can still recall the shock-wave when in 1934 work was stopped on the QUEEN MARY, building in John Browns, due to lack of money but of course putting yet more men out of work. Conversely resumption of work on the ship some two years later was a tangible turning point on the fortunes of the industry and the economy of the region as a whole.

An undercurrent to the burgeoning industrial scene was an active social life; lots of golf, sailing, climbing and parties that myself and friends could indulge in freely or at a modest cost (membership of Troon Golf Club was £4 per annum). If one followed the news there was a presentiment that it would all end in tears and we discussed amongst ourselves which service we would favour when it came to the crunch. Several friends joined the Territorials which never appealed to me following route marches with the OTC up and down hills clad in a kilt, heavy Army tunic and a rifle slung over one's shoulder. The RAF in the form of the Auxiliary Air Force certainly did; we had all been fired up at the exploit of the Duke of Hamilton's flight over Everest in 1934 when he was CO of 602 (City of Glasgow) Squadron based at Abbotsinch. My great friend Willis Roxburgh and I, on applying to join in about 1936, were interviewed by him and other officers several of whom we knew personally and were duly accepted. However, we were both under 21 and as the application form had to be signed by a parent it wasn't long before our fathers spoke together on the phone and jointly vetoed the project. In due course Willis did join the RAF, flying in Coastal Command and came through safely with a DFC: not many of 602 Squadron survived.

So it was the Navy for me. About 1937 their Lordships realised the Navy would have to be expanded quickly and there were not enough Reserve officers in the long established regular RNVR to meet the requirement. My brother Kenneth had joined some time before and by then was a Midshipman; he had done some seagoing training and regular instruction at the excellent RNVR Headquarters at Copelaw Street in Govan.

To meet the shortage a List II RNVR was authorised - a vigorous recruitment campaign, headed by Cdr Maurice Clark RNVR, CO of the Clyde Division, was put in place. The qualifications were obscure but seemed mainly to consist of which end of a sailing boat was the bow or stern and how to use a knife and fork. This trawl suited me well and after a day at sea in Maurice Clark's beautiful yacht VADURA, and an interview with the Duke of Montrose, Commodore of the Clyde Division, who had been a powerful figure in maintaining the continuity of the RNVR between the wars, I was signed on. As I was 23 at the time I was given two wavy stripes which later became an embarrassment when I was appointed to a cruiser and my colossal ignorance of all things Naval was exposed. My seniority as a Lieutenant was later confirmed as 24th May 1939. Apart from being alerted at the time of the 1938 Munich Crisis with Germany, we could not do much training as the facilities and staff at Clyde Division Headquarters were fully occupied with the Regular RNVR training.

Although I did not appreciate it at the time, as I never dreamt the duration of the war would be six years, there was another built-in benefit of joining the Navy; apart from always being close to my B and B, however far I roamed my ship would almost certainly return to the UK at some time or another giving me the opportunity for some leave at home. By contrast many of my contemporaries who joined the Army spent years in the uncomfortable sands of the desert or the hot unfriendly jungles of the East.

My brother James was not allowed to join up as he was in a reserved occupation with the family marine insulation company and our elderly father needed his help. He would dearly have loved to join the Navy as his great love was sailing and he would never have an engine in any of his boats. He was a wild-side character; he didn't drink or smoke but one of his after dinner party tricks was to drive his Austin Seven between two tram cars as they were passing each other and, incidentally, he was always keen to prove to any girl that there were 12 positions in his Austin Seven. At the outbreak of war he became a Special Constable with the Glasgow Police - arguably as dangerous as going to war!

Meanwhile civilian life went on as usual. Uncle Alan McCulloch had died in 1938 and Uncle John was getting pretty shaky and sherry-addicted; so the responsibility for the engineering merchant business of A & J McCulloch which, in the circumstances referred to earlier, was doing well, fell more and more to me.

An aspect of this business was our connection with the German firm of Rhurstahl AG based near Dusseldorf for whom we were the UK agents selling their heavy forgings for marine diesel engines and propeller shafts to the Clyde and NE Coast shipyards. In 1938 I visited Rhurstahl in company with Uncle Alan and, to add to the uneasiness absorbed from newspaper reports of developments in Germany, we found a strange frenetic atmosphere wherever we went. We travelled to the great trade fair at Leipzig and to Berlin as well as Dusseldorf. The German Army seemed to be everywhere and you certainly had to step aside if not get off the pavement as they arrogantly strode along.

At the border crossing into Germany the train stopped for ages as an army of 'Grenz-polizei' (customs officials) in army-style uniforms and revolvers swept along the train examining everyone's luggage and confiscating cigarettes. Practising my German on them I asked *"Why cigarettes?"* and they replied they were for *"Kriegsgeblindeten Soldaten"*. No one protested at this blatant rip-off.

In our hotel in Berlin I had run into Arthur Brown, an acquaintance from Glasgow. One evening, when Uncle Alan had turned in, I met him in the lobby and off we went to one of the notorious night clubs on Unter den Linden where our innocent Scottish eyes were opened to some nasty Aryan decadence.

In April 1939 I went to Norway with brother, Jimmy. We sailed in the VEGA to Bergen and then went for a week's skiing at Finse, which was an improvement on clattering down the rocks of Ben Lawers, and we enjoyed brilliant weather too. However, there were no ski-lifts and one still had to climb every foot one slid down. There were fun people in the hotel, especially the blonde barmaids whom one met coming down the mountains the next morning as one climbed up! Baron, the society photographer who was on a commission from the Norwegian Royal Family, was one of the guests and I still have a picture he took of me on the BLACK PRINCE coming home from Stavanger. I came across this ship later in the war when she had become a Commando headquarters ship.

1939 was a summer of glorious weather and Kirsteen and I made the most of it. She had joined the newly formed Women's Auxiliary Air Force and had been to London for interviews as 'potential officer material'. In the event she didn't qualify as at 19 she was too young! Her sister Jocelyn, two years older, received a commission and on the outbreak of the war both were posted to the RAF Marine Experimental Station at Rhu on the Gareloch where Kirsteen maintained and drove enormous WWI trucks and Jocelyn swanned it in the Officers Mess! Before being posted there she and her friends spent weeks filling cartridge belts for 602 Squadron's planes. By all accounts they were well looked after by the pilots, many of whom she knew.

In August of 1939 the Orr family, who at that time had moved to Ayr, were holidaying at St. Andrews, staying at 52 North Street, an address I will never forget as it became a target for a stream of letters when I was uprooted and dispatched over the horizon. At weekends I cut away from the office in 140 West George Street in Glasgow as early as I could on Friday evenings and sped through to St Andrews. On the way I usually stopped at a roadside phone box[1] in Carnbo to plug in and shave (to remove my 5 o'clock shadow) with my electric Sunbeam razor - hi-tech in those days!

Saturday 19th August was a drizzly day with a coastal haar ruling out golf so Kirsteen and I went off in the car to Crail where on Lundin Links I popped 'The Question', returning to St. Andrews where we duly celebrated. It was no surprise to the family. My parents had gone off on a Mediterranean cruise and couldn't be contacted. Next morning brother James arrived through from the West with a priority telegram from the Admiralty - as the holiday house had no telephone. Content *"You are appointed HMS DORSETSHIRE in Hong Kong. Report RNVR Headquarters for further instructions"*. The further instructions were to join HMT[2] DUNERA in Southampton by noon on Friday 25th August. This gave me three days to sort out my personal and business affairs and collect together what extra uniform, including tropical kit, I would need. There were important things like engagement rings and wills to be dealt with: my engagement present from Kirsteen of ivory hairbrushes I still have today; and the Rolex Oyster[3] from Uncle John McCulloch likewise ticks away. Not so Uncle John himself in spite of me phoning his doctor, Arthur Innes, to ask for him to be kept alive until I returned. Like 1914 we all expected the war to be over by Christmas. In the course of all the dashing around to accomplish this I crashed my precious SS Jaguar near my home. I told the local attendant Bobby I was off to

---

[1] There to this day.

[2] His Majesty's Transportship

[3] As Naval Officers at that time did not have Personal Numbers, this watch is engraved with my name, rank and 'C of S' to replicate a 'dog-tag'.

the war and he would have to deal with it, at which juncture I walked home! In the event Jimmy sorted it out but I never saw the car again.

Kirsteen organised a farewell party at Erskine Avenue on the Wednesday night which is memorable to this day. Their signatures are recorded inside my naval 'Solar Bowler' which was worn once in six years and has survived!

So to the night sleeper from Glasgow Central Station on Thursday 24th August, where the families of the Clyde Division detachment sailing on the DUNERA had gathered to see us off. Kirsteen, Jimmie, Kenneth and a tearful Uncle John McCulloch, who had served in the RNVR minelayers in World War I, bundled me on to the train complete with enough luggage to emigrate – including, believe it or not, my golf clubs which I ended up using in some interesting places. Lord Cardigan did, after all, take his yacht to the Crimean War.

We sailed at 1400 from Southampton escorted by the cruisers DAUNTLESS and EXETER and made for Gibraltar at 15 knots. The Clyde Detachment, consisting of Bob Pattman, James Matheson and Douglas Watson going to the minesweepers ABERDARE and HUNTLEY at Singapore; Alick Kennedy to MTBs in Hong Kong; Charlie Dobson to the old WWI destroyer THRACIAN in Hong Kong; and myself to the 8" gun County Class cruiser DORSETSHIRE of the Pacific Fleet's 5th Cruiser Squadron, China Station, based in Hong Kong and Weihaiwei. I don't know what happened to Watson, but Pattman and Jimmie Matheson slipped away ahead of the Japs. Jimmie on return to the UK went into Coastal Forces to become an admired genius at their training establishment, HMS BEE. He eventually organised the ML/MTB involvement in Operation OVERLORD, the D-Day landings. Post war he became my stockbroker! Alick Kennedy had a spectacular escape from Hong Kong with several of the crew of his MTB, always just a step ahead of the Japs and returned to the UK travelling through mainland China by bus and on foot to Lashio, Mandalay, the Burma Road and on to Rangoon. After many adventures he took passage to Arakan; then via Calcutta, Bombay and Cape Town finally arriving back on the Clyde on the same day, 24th May 1942, as his fiancée Rachel

Smith, daughter of the Acting Governor of Hong Kong A K Smith. Rachel and her family had also escaped from Hong Kong to Australia. After safely crossing the Pacific and passing through the Panama Canal, their ship was torpedoed off the Florida coast. Rescued, they too finally reached the Clyde. This amazing story is recounted in Alick's book 'Hong Kong Full Circle'[4].

Back to my tale. We reached Gibraltar by Tuesday 29th August and had a run ashore including a visit to the Rock Hotel with the 'Clydes' as well as trying to get missing bits of tropical uniform that we couldn't track down in Glasgow. We sailed that night with strong rumours that the pocket battleship ADMIRAL GRAF SPEE was in the vicinity, a fact I later established to be true. She had left Kiel on 21st August and was in the North Atlantic with orders to attack merchant shipping but to avoid confrontation with Allied warships. However, we went on through the Mediterranean to Malta where we made a quick stop in Valetta to drop off a naval draft and then on to Port Said and the Suez Canal. We were approaching Port Said in early September when war was declared on the 3rd and the awful news came of the torpedoing of the SS ATHENIA in the Western Approaches; there was no 'phoney war' for the Navy. At a further quick bus stop visit to Aden on the 11th we dropped off another draft. All this time classes in navigation and other obscure naval disciplines were organised for the ignorant RNVR officers by regular RN officers; these were eagerly attended. On to Colombo for a couple of delightful days of 'runs ashore' to the town and the very civilised 'Raj' style Galle Face Hotel where we dined well and swam.

[4] 'Hong Kong' Full Circle 1939-45, Lt Cdr Alexander Kennedy VRD RNVR, privately published. Printed by Harrison & Son, London 1970.

GUESTS AT THE FAREWELL PARTY
3 ERSKINE AVENUE
Wednesday 23rd August 1939

+ Kirsteen Orr	Engaged to yours truly, WAAF
+ Jimmy Miller	Elder brother
+ Kenneth Miller	Younger brother, Midshipman Clyde Division RNVR
Jocelyn Orr	Kirsteen's elder sister, Flying officer WAAF
Terry Easton	Sub-Lieutenant Clyde Division RNVR
+ Charlie Dobson	Midshipman Clyde Division RNVR, prisoner of Japanese in Hong Kong, Commanded Clyde Division RNVR after the war
Alick Kennedy	Sub-Lieutenant RNVR, escaped Hong Kong ahead of the Japanese, author of *Hong Kong Full Circle*
+ Norman Cadzow	Lieutenant Clyde Division RNVR
Cargill Sandeman	Sub-Lieutenant Clyde Division RNVR
+ Lyndsay Mavor	Married Cargill Sandeman 1941, VAD
Ruby White	VAD, entered Belsen with first British troops in 1945
+ Jim Gilmour	Pay Lieutenant Clyde Division RNVR
Betty Walker	Married Bernie Brown!
Paddy Davis	Clyde Division RNVR
Douglas Watson	Clyde Division RNVR

+ Died before end of 1996

We reached Singapore by the 24th September where we went alongside the Johore Naval Base. It didn't take Alick Kennedy, Charlie Dobson, Davey and myself long to organise a taxi for the 18 miles into town and the renowned attractions of Raffles Hotel. Life there seemed very undisturbed by the war in the West and we had an enjoyable six days while waiting for our next transport, HMT ETTRICK, to arrive from Hong Kong and take us back there. The detachment was now much smaller and we all had fine cabins on 'A' Deck and a Marine servant! After a lengthy roundabout voyage, which seemed an endless poker game, we reached Hong Kong on 6th October 1939. I was entranced by the lovely islands and the vibrant atmosphere ashore and afloat - hundreds of junks scurrying back and forth across the harbour and around the coast at Kowloon. The present denizens would consider it peaceful and quiet. I was lucky to have a week on the Island staying at their Lordships pleasure at the Gloucester Hotel and being lent a car by Lt R R W Ashby of Jardine Matheson and the Hong Kong RNVR - the usual family introduction. Ashby escaped from Hong Kong just ahead of the Japanese and had a brilliant career in MTB's in the Channel being awarded the DSC.

DORSETSHIRE arrived on Friday 13th October and I hoped not to sail that inauspicious day! I joined a.m. on the 14th but she was going in for a scrub and a paint at Whampoa Dock so we didn't sail until the 20th. The days were pleasantly filled making the most of visits to Repulse Bay and the delights of Hong Kong. All the officers and men leaped ashore to their favourite haunts whenever duties allowed.

The Repulse Bay Hotel was known as the 'Honeymoon Hotel of the East', and it was indeed a lovely place: writing to Kirsteen I promised her we would have our honeymoon there. In the event we did make it in 1962 when building my boat 'CHINA CLIPPER' at the Wing On Shing Shipyard in Kowloon, just in time to see the hotel being pulled down to build a block of flats!

It was a useful opportunity for me to settle down aboard as it was all very strange with the ship in a relaxed state with half the crew on shore leave at any one time. Apart from attending on the Captain when summoned to report joining ship, the most formal event was an inspection visit from the CinC China Station, Admiral Sir Percy Noble, dressed in gorgeous white shark-skin uniform, red-faced and popeyed. Going down the line of officers he stopped opposite me with my RNVR stripes, turned to Capt Martin and said *"These are the fellows who are going to run the Navy this war; make sure they are well trained"*. This was the spur which gave me access to and help from the core of highly professional naval officers on board, in all the disciplines I would need. I also sat in with the midshipmen in the gunroom when they were having instruction from the 'schoolie' - Lt G Britton.

Our CO, Capt BCS Martin RN, was an interesting character: he had joined the Navy as a boy and worked his way up through the hawse-pipe by intelligence and force of personality. Perforce he had a narrow outlook focussed on the Navy. The apogee of his career was the final sinking of the BISMARCK for which he won a well deserved DSO and was promoted Rear-Admiral, eventually retiring to Durban.

We sailed from Hong Kong on 20th October heading for Singapore where we berthed and oiled at Johore Naval Base to form part of Force 'I' with the aircraft carrier EAGLE and our sister ship CORNWALL. From there we went to Colombo and lots of exercises with CORNWALL, EAGLE and GLOUCESTER with full calibre 8" gun shoots as well as 4" high angle (HA) anti-aircraft shooting practice at drogues, towed by our amphibious Walrus aircraft known as a 'shagbat'. We had one glorious day off when we anchored at Ihavandiffulu Atoll in the Maldive Islands and, taking a cutter with some lieutenants and midshipmen, had a picnic ashore.

Meanwhile signals were keeping us informed of the likely whereabouts and activities of the pocket battleships GRAF SPEE, VON SCHEER and DEUTSCHLAND roving the North and South Atlantic preying on shipping. The whole scene was hotting up. We were brought sharply to reality when the AFRICA SHELL, a small British tanker, was sunk by the GRAF SPEE on 15th November just north of Lourenço Marques. This was on our patch.

Chapter II

HMS DORSETSHIRE
November 1939 – March 1940

From about the middle of November 1939 the naval war in the South Atlantic and Indian Ocean moved into top gear. It is an enormous area ranging from the Equator to the ice of the Antarctic. Little is commonly known of the battles and pursuits that were waged there apart from the spectacular and successful destruction of the GRAF SPEE off the River Plate by the EXETER, ACHILLES and AJAX on 13th December 1939.

As a young RNVR lieutenant on HMS DORSETSHIRE, I only saw one side of this far flung campaign while the ship was diverted hither and thither for thousands of miles in response to the latest signals from the Admiralty following the sinking of an Allied freighter or 'appreciation of the situation' of the commerce raiders in the area.

At that period of the war U-boats were not a threat on the trade routes South of the equator: and it was not until April 1941 that two U-boats operated beyond Freetown, Sierra Leone. Having said that, captains of cruisers such as DORSETSHIRE were rightly paranoid about U-boats as their ships were large and easy targets with no means of defence to either detect or attack them. Consequently we zigzagged every 20 minutes of the day if we were patrolling at 20 knots or below. Rescue work by cruisers that had arrived on the scene of a merchant ship sunk by a U-boat was often criticised by the survivors for abandoning them. If there was any suspicion that a U-boat was still around, the cruiser simply couldn't hang around and invite another torpedo. It was different with destroyers and smaller warships who had counter-measures for U-boats.

As the perceived threat at this juncture was the known presence of the powerful pocket battleships in the North and South Atlantic, with their potential to disrupt the trade routes to South America and round the Cape of Good Hope to the Indian Ocean and the East, the Admiralty and French Ministry of Marine formed their cruiser fleet into eight groups of three cruisers. An option was to replace a cruiser with one of our few aircraft carriers, and this grouping was considered strong enough to take on a single German pocket battleship. Hence our unit was Force 'I' consisting of DORSETSHIRE, CORNWALL and the aircraft carrier HMS EAGLE, which during 1930 was being built in the UK as a battleship for the Chilean Navy before being requisitioned by the Admiralty and completed as a carrier. As part of this strategy we were based on Colombo and constantly exercised tactics to confront a pocket battleship should the occasion arise. On 3rd December we were detached from Force 'I' and after oiling at Mauritius set off at 28 knots for Simons Town. When I was on night watch on the plot the Captain came in with a decrypted signal from the Admiralty and took out a chart of the world! He drew lines that indicated we would be in the Falkland Isles by Christmas after which we would patrol the east coast of South America as far north as Pernambuco. We made Simons Town by the 9th and had a few lovely days ashore at the Cape before setting off towards Tristan da Cunha on the 13th in a strong south-easterly and enormous seas around Agulhas. News of the GRAF SPEE's battle off Montevideo was coming through. I was getting reports direct from the American radio network NBC on the powerful Phillips radio I had bought in Colombo and had in my cabin, with an aerial rigged out of my porthole and attached to the guardrail above. The NBC had 5 observers along the Uruguayan coast with radio links to the USA waiting for the battle to resume. As I intercepted this link I heard the NBC man in New York tell his man in Montevideo that he had 107 stations standing by across the US waiting for the GRAF SPEE to leave harbour and continue the battle. It was the most exciting broadcast I have ever heard.

Meanwhile our proposed visit to Tristan da Cunha was cancelled and we set off from Simons Town at full speed on the 13th on a Great Circle course for the River Plate and Montevideo, with the world waiting for Admiral Langsdorf's decision whether to come out and fight or not. Our engineer, Commander Buttar, wound DORSETSHIRE up to 36 knots; the funnels glowed red in the night as I stood watch. There was much speculation on the BBC, which was embroidered by the broadcasts I was intercepting from the NBC in the USA. Two different stories emerged. Disinformation from the Admiralty had it that the ARK ROYAL, RENOWN and the 2nd Destroyer Flotilla (DF) were more or less standing off the River Plate already waiting for the GRAF SPEE, whereas in fact they were some 900 miles away. The 8" County Class cruiser HMS CUMBERLAND, up from the Falkland Isles, had certainly joined AJAX and ACHILLES and would probably have been a sufficient force to have seen off the damaged GRAF SPEE. HMS EXETER was badly damaged and already on her way to the Falklands to lick her wounds.

In the event, of course, the GRAF SPEE scuttled herself five miles off Montevideo on 17th December with Capt Langsdorf committing suicide. Incidentally, Langsdorf, since leaving Wilhelmshaven on 21st August 1939 in command of the GRAF SPEE, had destroyed nine British ships; and until she was caught off the River Plate had not caused the loss of one British life from the merchantmen sunk. Some of the 300 prisoners from these ships had been transferred to the notorious oiler and supply ship ALTMARK which, as part of the organisation to support the GRAF SPEE and other raiders, had topped up with oil at Port Arthur in Texas on 19th August. She refuelled the GRAF SPEE on 14th October and 6th December as well as relieving her of prisoners. The ALTMARK was eventually caught on 16th February 1940 by the Tribal Class destroyer COSSACK in a spectacular boarding rescue by Captain Vian off southern Norway shortly before reaching Germany, and the prisoners were liberated.

A shuffling of the pack after the Plate battle moved us to Force G with HMS SHROPSHIRE with our Capt Martin as Senior Officer. This he loved and even set up a special office for the function!

With the GRAF SPEE out of the way and no other German pocket battleship or warship as yet south of the equator our objectives altered slightly. Firstly there were a number of German merchantmen holed up in South American ports waiting for an opportunity to break out and head for home. The Admiralty kept us posted with their names and presumably our embassies and consulates patrolled the docksides to monitor and report on pending sailings. At the same time we oiled and topped up with supplies from fleet auxiliaries such as the OLWEN outside the 3 mile limit.

After several abortive pursuits of these ships we did catch the German WAKAMA which had slipped out of Rio de Janeiro at 1 a.m. on 12th February 1940. We chased her from the south at 25 knots, sending up the Walrus aircraft twice and on the second flight we found her. The crew abandoned ship in two sailing lifeboats after setting fire to her and when we had recovered the Walrus at 1750 we picked up the 10 officers, 26 men, 2 cats and a canary. We used the burning ship as target practice for the 8" and 4" armament and sank her at 2115. Immediately afterwards we set off to cover Santos near Rio for the reported imminent sailing of the Nazi WINDHUK.

The badly damaged EXETER together with ACHILLES and AJAX had made for the Falklands. After a few days patrolling off the River Plate with CUMBERLAND we both oiled from the Fleet oiler CAPULET and together set off to the Falklands where we arrived on Christmas Eve, Sunday December 24th 1939. CUMBERLAND collected mail from all the ships in Port Stanley and set off for Simons Town some 3500 miles by Great Circle to collect three Harley Street surgeons being flown out by an Imperial Airways flying boat to Cape Town. There they transferred to CUMBERLAND, to then be sailed to the Falklands to minister to the wounded on EXETER. One such, drafted to DORSETSHIRE, was a Mr B B Moroney who had a metamorphosis into Surg-Cdr RNVR and subsequently had difficulty restraining an urge to shake hands with the Officer of the Watch when he went over the side. The hospital at Port Stanley and the ships' sick bays, including ours on DORSETSHIRE, were full of the wounded; some with awful injuries.

So to a strange Christmas 1939 at the Falkland Isles, ostensibly summertime there but as windy and cold as Scotland in winter with a constant threat of sleet or snow. After listening to the King's speech we took a party in the pinnace round EXETER, ACHILLES and AJAX and gave them a 'chukka'. EXETER cleared lower deck and returned the cheers. On ACHILLES the corpulent newly promoted Admiral Harwood (ex-Commodore) in his new brass hat gave us a return cheer. Because of short notice for sea and the dreadful weather there was no shore leave and we amused ourselves by organising a concert for the troops. The oiler CAPULET had been dragging her anchor in Stanley Harbour for about two days and nearly hit us. She asked for medical assistance for a sick sailor and I was sent off in charge of a cutter with Doc Martin and sick-bay attendants all weighed down in duffle-coats and lifebelts; the outcome being that we were blown onto a lee shore with the crew exhausted. I had taken over an oar after one rating collapsed.

With waves breaking over us and myself in stocking soles having lost a seaboot clambering over the rocks we managed to secure the cutter behind a reef. The men went ashore and lit a fire to dry and warm themselves and succeeded in setting the peat alight! DORSETSHIRE paid out another cutter on a grass line and towed us off further along the shore. I had lost my cap and was exhausted. The Captain bollocked me for not returning to the ship when the recall signal was hoisted! However, he and the Commander did congratulate me on the way I had handled and secured the boat. The illness case on CAPULET was dealt with from CUMBERLAND in a power-boat which should have been used in the first place. Our cutter was recovered undamaged when the weather abated.

We sailed on the 29th in company with CUMBERLAND on her way to Simons Town without ever having put a foot ashore on the Falklands and resumed our patrol off the South American coast on the lookout for German merchant ships such as the TACOMA, reported as preparing to sail from Montevideo. On 5th January we were in the estuary of the River Plate about 3 miles off Montevideo and went in close to have a look at the sunken GRAF SPEE with her exposed upper works already looking rusty and old after the fire. We circled her and stopped about 3 cables off to lower a pinnace with our navigator, Cdr

Westmacott, and radio technician aboard. They went alongside the forward mast structure to climb up it to the radar display and measure the length of the radar antenna. This information was duly flashed to the Admiralty. This enabled our experts at home to confirm the wavelength the Germans were using for their naval radar range-finding; it was one and a half metres.

On joining up with SHROPSHIRE, ACHILLES and AJAX from time to time we continued our patrolling as far north as Rio de Janeiro with AJAX going in for a well-deserved 24 hour propaganda fling. The only merit in these activities was that the weather was warm and we were in tropical rig.

This didn't last long: on the 16th we were heading again for the Falklands and into blues and duffle-coats. When we got there on the 18th poor EXETER was still in Port Stanley. Still there was no shore leave on account of the weather but at last the wind abated and the sailors hit the beach for the first time in about two months. I put in lots of walking with Kenneth Martin, the RNVR Doctor. On the 21st we sailed with the damaged EXETER to escort her at 14 knots to join up with ARK ROYAL and RENOWN (Force K) who were to take over for the passage home. As we parted we passed her with our Marine band playing and gave her a big cheer.

The rather dull routine of blockading the neutral South American ports was lifted by a long awaited visit to one of them. On 8th February 1940 we entered the muddy waters of the River Plate at 0500, heading for Buenos Aires where we went alongside at 1500 with a huge crowd to welcome us and a programme of activities prepared by the British community for the entertainment of the whole crew when off watch. I was whisked off with John Westmacott (newly promoted Commander) to golf at the Argentine Golf Club where we were looked after and played with Jose Jurado whom I had seen playing in 1931 at Carnoustie when he was runner-up to Tommy Armour in the Open Championship. This was a great start to a sleepless 24-hours of non-stop high jinks. We had a drinks party at the English Club, dinner at some restaurant, a dance elsewhere, then on to The Tabaris night-club, getting back on board about 0500 to read my mail. I then went on watch on the Quarterdeck at 0800 in No 1 Whites complete with solar bowler and telescope[5] under my oxter! I received Ambassador Ovey on board at noon and then, after handing over to Harry Parker, sloped off to the Jockey Club for lunch. Thankfully we sailed at 1700.

A notable feature of Buenos Aires was the number of the interned crew of the GRAF SPEE wandering about and coming down to the docks to have a look at us. Argentina was of course neutral but in contrast to Uruguay had pro-German sympathies and offered hospitality to many internees. Also that once again very welcome mail was waiting for us on arrival at Buenos Aires. I never ceased to be amazed, in view of our apparently haphazard wanderings in the southern oceans, how the GPO London managed to have the elixir of mail waiting for us wherever we touched down.

It was from Buenos Aires on 10th February that we sailed and caught the WAKANA on 12th February as described earlier. We had her prisoners on board until we reached Cape Town on 11th March. They were very well behaved and seemed to be glad to be out of the war in comfortable South Africa. The patrol area from the Plate to Pernambuco and eastwards to St Helena and Ascension occupied us for a few weeks in company with HAWKINS and a rendezvous with the AMC[6] QUEEN OF BERMUDA to exchange mail: then she went into Rio for 24 hours. She was a lovely ship but would have been useless as a warship in a fight. Eventually we got the inevitable signal to head for the Falklands again which amongst other discomforts meant 'blues' replaced tropical 'whites'. Arriving on the 29th February we had for the first time some pleasant days ashore including dinner with the schoolteachers at the School House and some quiet drinks at the club. Again an unexpected mail arrived which rounded off the visit. Some of the sailors got roaring drunk on beer laced with rum and were in deep trouble! There was a dance in the evening with the Governor's daughter attending[7].

[5] The Officer of the Watch's badge of office.

[6] Armed Merchant Cruiser

[7] The same evening HE The Governor entertained other officers to drinks at Government House. My son, AK, obtained a copy of the relevant page of the Visitors Book from the Falkland Islands' Museum in Stanley whilst on a battlefield tour in Dec 96.

And so off to Simons Town on 2nd March by Great Circle but avoiding the Antarctic ice with some of EXETER's wounded who were on board to be landed at Cape Town. We paused at Tristan da Cunha at dawn on the 7th. The main island rises to 7000 feet with streaks of mist in layers around the top and a group of smaller islands lie to the south. We swung into the settlement about 0930 and a boat sailed out with the Reverend Minister and others aboard. He had distinct symptoms of scurvy and went to the sick bay for examination and presumably some vitamins from the Doc. The island looked scrubby with potato patches, crofts and a number of boats around the village fishing. We loaded up their boat with books, wood and tinned food. The 130-odd islanders were presumed descendants of the Cape Coloureds who were imported to comfort the Marine Garrison at the time of the Napoleonic wars.

After a middle watch, I awoke to a marvellous view of Table Mountain in the dawn of 11th March, with all the delights of Cape Town in prospect. Mail was waiting by the usual appreciated magic. As we expected to be in dock at Simons Town for some time I shared the purchase at £22.10/- of a yellow De Soto roadster (the Yellow Peril) with Ken Martin - we were mobile (!) - and kept her in the Dockyard. An active life ensued - squash, golf, mostly at Mowbray and Royal Cape, with parties and dances laid on for us. On Sunday 17th March, after a game of squash in the morning, I climbed Table Mountain with Bill Tyndale-Biscoe, the Marine Lieutenant. The 'table-cloth' mist came over when we reached the top but it was a grand climb and as good a day as I'd had since leaving Scotland. On the way up from the Kirstenbosch side we ran into General Smuts and his friends coming down in the course of his regular Sunday outing. He was instantly recognisable by his goatee beard. Inevitably a number of friendships were made: with the Vineys, she being the S.A. Ladies champion golfer, and he an Old Milhillian; the Duncans, also golfers: he was a Lt Col and CO of the volunteer Cape Town Highlanders, to be tragically killed in Italy in the last week of the war; the Newton-Thompsons, their son a pre-war rugby player for Cambridge University who took me to Stellenbosch Afrikaans University and other places of interest. By a strange coincidence I met his widow in Cape Town for the first time 57 years later. Mrs Newton-Thompson senior had been a suffragette with Mrs Pankhurst in London. Another highlight of this shoreside interlude were tennis (not my game!) at Kelvingrove partnering Jan Hoffmeyer, the South African Finance Minister, against the University Vice-Chancellor Faulkner and AN Other: I leapt about like an impala! Early on in the visit to Simons Town I had also met a young South African 'Ginger' Brukman and his merry band of rugby playing friends who thereafter included me in their parties. He played a squeeze-box and needed little encouragement to start up a party with it. He had a printing business and although I had never heard of Bell's Asbestos at that time I learned after the war when I went to South Africa on business that he published their catalogue; his firm was South African Office Supplies Co.

On the naval front, the QUEEN MARY and AQUITANIA arrived in Cape Town on their way to Australia to collect troops for the Middle East. Some of us went out in an Asdic-fitted trawler, the BLOUVEI, in the most enormous seas to Cape Hangklip at the entrance to False Bay to test the gear and hopefully obtain some practice. It was too rough and all the crew were sick; we did anchor in the lee of the Point and caught millions of Silver and Hottentot fish.

News of the invasion of Norway and Denmark on 9th April sobered us all up and made us realise the war was probably beginning to spread throughout Europe.

We came out of dry-dock on 18th April and began squaring off the ship to get ready for sea. Glistening with new paint, DORSETSHIRE sailed on the 24th and rounded the Cape of Good Hope at 20 knots on the way to Freetown, Sierra Leone.

It sounds as though it was all fun and games in Cape Town but we did in fact have our duties on board and spent a lot of time organising activities for the crew such as football matches against local teams and other ships in harbour as well as visits up country.

Chapter III

GERMAN COMMERCE RAIDERS
RAIDER 45 – 'KOMET'
March – June 1940

The three pocket-battleships, GRAF SPEE, ADMIRAL SCHEER and DEUTSCHLAND had all left Germany in August 1939 to take up their operational areas and were ordered on 26th September to attack British shipping. The DEUTSCHLAND did not achieve much and, after the unhappy and shocking precedent of the GRAF SPEE, was withdrawn by Admiral Raeder to Germany following pressure by Hitler that it would be bad for the country's morale if a ship of that name was sunk like the GRAF SPEE; eventually her name was changed to the LUTZOW! She never operated as a commerce raider again.

However, although the ADMIRAL SCHEER did not spend long on her first sortie in 1939, she re-emerged on 28th October 1940 and had an effective cruise in the North and South Atlantic and Indian Ocean sinking HMS JERVIS BAY, an A.M.C., in an heroic defensive action, and then some sixteen merchant ships before returning to Bergen on 30th March 1941. The 8" gun HIPPER was also loose at that time but only sank one ship before returning to Bremen on 27th December 1940.

And so our theatre was free of the powerful pocket-battleships for the time being but another unforeseen force was beginning to make its presence felt. This was an unorthodox fleet of disguised merchant raiders called 'auxiliary cruisers' by the Germans; similar ships had been quite successful in the Great War and, apparently this fleet, unknown to the Allies, had now been under conversion for many months in Germany. These ships were fairly fast merchant ships armed with six to eight 5.9" guns, a small secondary armament, and at least two torpedo tubes, so their fire-power would enable them to confront a 6" cruiser if necessary although their rules of engagement, like the pocket-battleship, were to avoid such action if possible. Some of the later vessels of this fleet even carried a couple of small reconnaissance seaplanes and a motor torpedo boat to be launched in pursuit of the faster merchant ships; others were equipped as minelayers. The ships carried a crew of about 350 which included enough officers and seamen to provide prize crews for the ships they captured. Their captains were top of the list of experienced naval officers, well demonstrated by some of the brilliant successes they achieved.

Clever and elaborate disguise in the form of collapsible deckhouses, bulwarks, telescopic masts and funnels and extensive repainting could alter the basic appearance of the ship in days and transform her from a perceived merchantman of one national shipping line to a recognisable likeness of a vessel of another country. She would then approach a victim under false colours, an ancient naval ruse, before opening fire.

All this rapidly increasing secondary fleet began to make its mark from about March 1940 when the first disguised raider, the ATLANTIS, designated Ship No 16 by SKL (Seekriegsleitung), the operational arm of the OKM – Oberkommando der Marine - sailed for the Cape and Indian Ocean, to be followed by the ORION (Ship No 36) on 6th April 1940 who made her way to the Pacific by way of Cape Horn. The Admiralty classified them as Raiders 'A', 'B', 'C', etc as of course their names or numbers were not known to us until after the war.

The organisation attendant on the commerce raiders was immense bearing in mind the Germans had not the advantage of world-wide Commonwealth bases which the Allies enjoyed; it included measures to beat the British blockade from Wilhelmhaven through the Denmark Straits, to the positioning of supply ships deep in the South Atlantic and Indian Ocean serving as oilers and prison ships for captured merchant ship crews. As these cruisers captured ships, they helped themselves to the stores and oil aboard before taking off the crews and sinking the vessel. Alternatively they would take her as a prize and send her back to Bordeaux or temporarily to one of the deep south rendezvous points.

ATLANTIS was first reported on 2nd May as a 'suspicious Japanese vessel' by the liner CITY OF EXETER 600 miles south east of St Helena and her description circulated by the Admiralty. She made off but next afternoon stopped and sank the 6000 ton SCIENTIST before heading for Cape Agulhas, the southernmost point of South Africa to lay her mines. This she did on 10th/11th May on a 20-mile arc from the lighthouse. Their presence was detected on the 13th when the lighthouse keeper reported a heavy explosion out at sea. Admiral Hallifax in charge of the South African Seaward Defence Force mustered all available minesweepers to deal with this and in the event no ship was ever damaged by mines from this field. The enormously rough seas off Agulhas probably accounted for most of the mines going adrift and thereby self-destructing. Another more effective minefield was laid by the raider PINGUIN (Ship No 33) and PASSAT, formerly the Norwegian tanker STORSTAD captured by PINGUIN with 12,000 tons of diesel oil aboard. On 12th October 1940 the PASSAT was sent with 100 mines and a prize crew of twenty-two to mine the Bass Strait. Together with PINGUIN their mines sank four ships in the Bass Straits and off Sydney.

This, however, is not a story of the activities of the fleet of German disguised commerce raiders but only one or two of their more outstanding exploits and successes that are worth recounting. These took place after I had left DORSETSHIRE in January 1941 for the UK and a posting to a destroyer. After months and months of quartering the Southern Oceans, and escorting precious troop convoys round the Cape to the Red Sea, DORSETSHIRE, now under the command of Capt A W S Agar VC, managed to trap and sink one of the supply ships, PYTHON, caught on 1st December 1940 rendering assistance to the crew of ATLANTIS (Ship No 16, Raider 'C'), which herself had been sunk by HMS DEVONSHIRE on 22nd November whilst servicing several U-boats with torpedoes and stores. The presence of these U-boats did not allow DORSETSHIRE or DEVONSHIRE to hang around and they were left to their own rescue arrangements. The crews of PYTHON and ATLANTIS after many adventures as passengers on U-boats and Italian submarines reached St Nazaire and were feted as heroes in Berlin by Admiral Raeder. Capt Rogge of ATLANTIS was awarded the Oak Leaves to the Iron Cross with Diamonds. ATLANTIS had been at sea for 622 days and sunk or captured 22 ships amounting to a total of 145,698 tons. With her capture a distinctive phase of the naval war came to an end.

Another remarkable raider was the KOMET (Ship No 45), classified as Raider 'B' in the annals of the Admiralty. She was rather small at 3200 tons but commanded by a Rear Admiral Robert Eyssen. She left Gdynia on 3rd July 1940 and made her way up the Norwegian coast to the Arctic Circle where she was assisted through the North-East Passage by three Russian ice-breakers (Germany was still pally with the Russians at that time), until she entered the Pacific Ocean through the Bering Straits in early September and took up her operational area on the shipping route between New Zealand and the Panama Canal. Later in March 1941 she met supply ships and had a rest period ashore at the Kerguelen Islands near the ice barrier in the south Indian Ocean. Back in the Pacific she cruised with success sinking two British ships and capturing one Dutchman with a precious cargo of rubber, tin and manganese, as far east as the Galapagos Islands. Eventually she set off round the Horn and arrived with her prize at Cherbourg on 26th November 1941and then went up Channel to arrive in the Elbe on the 30th.

I now go fast forward to October 1942 in my diary to round off this episode concerning KOMET. I was by then First Lieutenant of HMS BROCKLESBY, a Hunt Class destroyer based on Devonport. The Hunts were modern well-equipped 1000 ton warships with the latest in radar, Asdic, director controlled 4" HA guns, and anti-aircraft armament, but no torpedoes. On 12th October we had been out in the Channel on a practice shoot and returned to harbour at 1930 following a signal that we were to sail at 2030 as Senior Officer of a flotilla of four 'Hunts' consisting of FERNIE, TYNEDALE, and our 'chummy' ship, the Polish manned KRAKOWIAK, designated Group 'B' of the forces being assembled. Force 'A' consisted of five other 'Hunts': COTTESMORE, QUORN, ALBRIGHTON and the Norwegian manned GLAISDALE and ESKDALE. Two flotillas of torpedo carrying MTBs (Groups 'C' and 'D') were to accompany us.

The situation was that a German fast commerce raider had sailed from Flushing at midnight on 7th/8th October on a course to the west down channel at 16 knots escorted by four or five 'T' Class destroyers. This ship was our old elusive adversary KOMET from my DORSETSHIRE days in the South Atlantic. She had completed her refit in Germany and was now setting out for a further campaign on the high seas. Our underground intelligence in Germany and Holland must have been keeping an eye on her refit progress and alerted the Admiralty of the sailing date. Without success, attempts had been made to intercept her going down Channel but she made it to Le Havre without interruption. On the evening of the 13th KOMET sailed from there with her escort but was spotted by a Coastal Command aircraft in the Baie de la Seine. Due to her speed of 16 knots there was not time for the main force to intercept her before she could reach Cherbourg. Hoping she would run the gauntlet of her final danger area before making the Atlantic, Group 'A' was ordered at full speed to an intercepting position near Cap de la Hague, the westernmost point of the Cherbourg Peninsula, and Group 'B' (us) was directed as a back-up on a course towards the Channel Isles.

The MTBs followed as best they could on a very dark night in a moderate west wind but in the prevailing conditions couldn't keep up. Group 'C' of the MTBs consisted of the older type and as the other flotilla, Group 'D', was following them, the MTBs became separated from the destroyers and never made contact with the enemy. However a strange and fortuitous development unfolded. MTB 236, one of the faster boats, was positioned at the end of the line of MTBs as she was commanded by its First Lieutenant, a Sub-Lt Drayson standing in for his CO who was sick. He was very junior with little experience and it was his first time in command. In the conditions prevailing he became detached from all the boats ahead and consequently decided to head direct towards Cap de le Hague.

Meanwhile HMS COTTESMORE with Lt Cdr J C A Ingram in command, the Senior Officer of Group 'A', first sighted the enemy vessels shortly before one o'clock and his destroyers fired starshell to illuminate. The battle had begun and the five Hunt Class destroyers were engaged with their 4" guns. The German destroyers retaliated by firing torpedoes which were all avoided by the Hunts. The enemy now turned south towards the land and the protection of the shore batteries which had begun to fire with considerable accuracy.

It was at this juncture that MTB 236 came upon the scene. Heading towards Cap de la Hague, Drayson heard the sound of gunfire and saw starshell lighting up a group of ships so decided to slip in towards the shore to intercept anything that might be trying to slink away in the smoke and confusion of the battle. Suddenly he sighted the main target silhouetted by starshell, which was being heavily engaged by the Hunts and on fire, but still making about 15 knots. At about 500 yards range Drayson lined up and fired his two torpedoes, getting a clean hit on KOMET. As he started his engines and turned away to starboard under cover of a smoke screen he was hit by a shot from the enemy but had no casualties.

A few seconds later KOMET burst into flames and blew up. The Senior Officer Lt Cdr Ingram described thus: *"a violent explosion took place followed by another which dwarfed the previous one. Flames shot up at least four hundred feet and a great pall of smoke rose to a height of several thousand feet".* KOMET had been carrying mines for laying off harbours and on trade routes as on her previous cruise. She also had 351 officers and men on board sufficient to provide prize crews for captured ships; all of them now perished. Although the Group 'A' destroyers would certainly have seen off KOMET, the initiative and courage of young Sub Lt Drayson in MTB 236 providing the only vital torpedoes on the scene was brilliant. He was decorated with the DSC. Two of the enemy's 'T' Class destroyers were sunk and the remainder made off towards Cherbourg and the protection of the shore batteries. They had fired their torpedoes but hit nothing.

Meanwhile our Group 'B' Hunts about 30 miles west of Guernsey had seen the loom of the KOMET battle and bright flash of the explosion about an hour before, and were at 0215 speeding north-eastwards with the island of Sark abeam to port and the coast of France to starboard.

Leading the six Hunts in line ahead we had identified on radar a group of ships approaching an opposite course on which we immediately opened fire although by then the shore batteries had started firing quite accurately at us. The enemy convoy consisted of four escorts, probably 'R' boats or armed minesweepers and four good sized merchant vessels. They were apparently in considerable confusion when we disengaged as they were seen to be firing at each other.

Inexplicably, after our flotilla with their dominating fire power had scored many hits on the convoy and escorts and some were on fire, our Captain gave the order to disengage and set course for Devonport. Personally I was disappointed at this decision and many of the officers on board BROCKLESBY and the other Hunts thought we should have pressed home our commanding position and wiped out the enemy. From that moment I lost confidence in our captain, Lt Cdr Blackler RN, but as he was Senior Officer of Group 'B' none of the other Captains could do other than conform.

The next account of raiders in 1941 is of a 'brilliant malice aforethought' operation by the raider PINGUIN (Ship No 33, Raider 'F') commanded by Capt Kruder. PINGUIN was one of the most effective commerce raiders of their phantom fleet accounting for 17 Allied merchantmen plus capturing 11 whalers. She was fast at 17 knots which of course was progressively reduced by weed and barnacles the longer she was at sea, carried two fragile HE114 seaplanes, 300 mines for her own minelaying purposes plus torpedoes and mines to pass on to U-boats operating in the South Atlantic.

By December 1940 Capt Kruder in PINGUIN was in the vicinity of the Crozets and Kerguelen Island in freezing temperatures. Although nearly midsummer, icebergs were sighted. On the 18th the SKL informed him that the British/Norwegian whaling fleet was operating within a radius of 200 miles of South Georgia and naming the factory and supply ships there. He altered course to Bouvet Island towards the north-west and on the 23rd wireless traffic between units of the whaling fleet was intercepted. On the 27th R/T conversations in Norwegian were picked up. That night PINGUIN increased speed and cut through wide fields of floating ice and icebergs 50 metres high. His direction finding (D/F) of the radio traffic placed him 150 miles north of the whaling factory ship PELAGOS: there was a 7-8 NW gale blowing and high seas rolling.

On 1st January PELAGOS obligingly broadcast her position and indicated that a supply ship the SOLGLINT was due. She duly met with the other Norwegian factory ship OLE WEGGER and, while the two were lying alongside each other, the PINGUIN duly pounced. Not a shot was fired and Kruder warned the ships not to broadcast the 'RRR' or use the radio-telephone (R/T) to the whalers.

There was effectively no resistance and half an hour later both ships, which had provisions for 10 weeks but importantly had 7000 and 4000 tons of whale oil, were prizes. Four of the whale catchers were also captured but two escaped and the next night PINGUIN captured PELAGOS in the same manner except that the captain was ordered to recall his catchers and all seven were seized. PELAGOS with its crew of 210 had provisions for ten weeks - most useful to the raider - and 9500 tons of whale oil on board. On 16th January PINGUIN sent her prizes south, with prize crews aboard to a rendezvous and herself sailed 500 miles north west to make a lengthy report to SKL and so avoid revealing the position of her wonderful prizes.

On the 25th PELAGOS and SOLGLINT were ordered to Bordeaux where they arrived in March. PINGUIN took on fuel and provisions from OLE WEGGER and on 1st February escorted her and the eleven whale-catchers into the South Atlantic. Near St Helena the OLE WEGGER, in charge of a prize crew, with her ten whale-catchers was released to sail to French ports. Two of the whale-catchers scuttled themselves just before reaching Bordeaux. One catcher was retained, renamed ADJUTANT, and converted by the Germans into a minelayer to operate with KOMET off the South Australian coast. PINGUIN continued with her depredations but eventually was caught and sunk by HMS CORNWALL just north of the Seychelles in the Indian Ocean on 8th May 1941. Some 200 British and Lascar prisoners were lost in PINGUIN but CORNWALL rescued sixty German seaman, fifteen Lascars and nine British seamen. Capt Kruder went down with his ship.

The next remarkable and tragic episode of the German commerce raiders campaign involved the action between KORMORAN (Ship No 41, Raider 'G') and HMAS SYDNEY, the Australian 6" Town Class cruiser and a near sister ship to DORSETSHIRE.

The KORMORAN, commanded by Capt Detmers, had cruised in the Indian Ocean since leaving Germany in December 1940 and in 10 months picked off 11 Allied merchantmen totalling 68,000 tons before she met a supply ship, the KULMERLAND from whom she stored and oiled 1000 miles west of Fremantle on 24th October 1941. She had disguised herself as the Dutch STRAAT MALAKKA when on 19th November she met HMAS SYDNEY 200 miles off the west Australian coast.

SYDNEY challenged repeatedly for KORMORAN to make her secret call-sign letters but Detmers turned away into the setting sun and fudged the hoisting of the STRAAT MALAKKA's letters. SYDNEY ordered several times that they should be hoisted clear but made no attempt to contact her shore base to have the STRAAT MALAKKA's presence in the area verified - a routine precaution, nor did she launch her Walrus to make a closer recce. By 1630 she had closed to 1500 yards with all her guns and torpedo tubes trained on the phoney STRAAT MALAKKA. Detmers then dropped his gun screens and opened fire with four 5.9" guns, the first salvo wrecking SYDNEY's bridge, the second her Walrus carried between the funnels, while a torpedo put her forward turrets out of action. SYDNEY's first salvo missed but the next set KORMORAN's fuel tanks ablaze. The raider continued firing at point blank range; SYDNEY replying with her after turrets and firing all her torpedoes which missed. By 1700 KORMORAN lay stopped with engine-room ablaze and SYDNEY moved slowly away to the south-east with her bows deep in the water and covered in smoke. As the flames in KORMORAN approached her mine chambers Detmers abandoned ship at 2300 and twenty minutes later she blew up. 315 members of KORMORAN's crew including the captain reached the Australian coast in lifeboats. From HMAS SYDNEY there were no survivors nor was any trace of the ship ever found.

This dreadful tragedy on 19th November 1941 is inexplicable and inexcusable. SYDNEY held all the cards, superior speed and armament, an aircraft (which she never launched), 700 trained officers and men and by this time in the war a knowledge of the tactics and strengths and weaknesses of the Nazi commerce raider fleet. Any midshipman could have smelt a rat in the behaviour of the KORMORAN and a signal to Headquarters for a check on the STRAAT MALAKKA would quickly have exposed her ruse. By contrast Capt Detmers cleverly and coolly lured SYDNEY to her destruction.

These are a selection of episodes in the fascinating campaign of the German commerce raider fleet which lasted from early 1940 to about October 1943 when the last of the raiders, the MICHEL (Ship No 28, Raider 'H'), and one of the most successful having accounted for 17 ships totalling 122,000 tons, was torpedoed by the American submarine TARPON on 17th October, 60 miles from Japan in the Pacific.

So now I will return to my story...........

Chapter IV

SOUTH ATLANTIC – SECOND TOUR
June – December 1940

D uring DORSETSHIRE'S six weeks refitting in Simons Town there had been some changes in the ship's complement. The Commander, 'Mickey' Garnons-Williams, a competent intellectual rather than an executive, had been replaced by John Westmacott, recently the navigator, and promoted to Commander at the New Year. He in turn had been succeeded by Lt Cdr Brian Durant as the ship's navigator. The latter was extremely supportive in coaching me towards my watch-keeping certificate which I was naturally anxious to achieve as a reward for all the months ploughing the oceans. Post-war he lived close to us in Egerton Crescent, Knightsbridge and went on to become an Admiral. Garnons-Williams now a Captain confounded my assessment of him by successfully acting as Senior Naval Officer (SNO) of the naval assault forces for the invasion of Madagascar on 4th May 1942. A number of South African RNVR officers and men, about 80 in all, joined the ship and, apart from those lost when the DORSETSHIRE was sunk off Ceylon, served in the RN until the end of the war.

It was now towards the end of April 1940 and on the 27th on the passage north, we joined HMS GLOUCESTER escorting the whaling factory ship TAFELBERG and carried on to Freetown, Sierra Leone, arriving on the 1st May. Freetown was the unpleasant dark olive green base of our new boss CinC South Atlantic, Admiral Sir D'Oyle Lyon, flying his flag in the DUNOTTAR CASTLE, an ex-Union Castle mailboat. This was the first of many visits in the forthcoming months and became known as the place to *"oil, toil, yam and scram"* - yams being the revolting substitute for potatoes. However there was a grotty golf course with sand greens and pleasant swimming and surfing at Lumley Beach which made going ashore worthwhile if only for some exercise. CORNWALL and our old friend the aircraft carrier HERMES were in port and we regularly went out exercising with them which was welcome as a breath of fresh air in contrast to Freetown Harbour.

The war at home took another turn for the worse with Holland, Belgium and France being invaded by the Nazis. Churchill ousted Chamberlain as Prime Minister. The Phillips radio in my cabin again proved its usefulness enabling me to keep in touch with world-wide news.

On 15th May we (that is, the junior ranks) unexpectedly sailed at 2.30 am from Freetown in company with CORNWALL for Gibraltar - excitement ran through the ship as this routing had the potential of a visit to the UK in the wake of the confusion surrounding the fate of the French fleet and the uncertainty of Italy's probable entry into the war.

I had had a splendid dinner on board HERMES with Bill McLachlan after a day sailing in the whaler and too much giggle-water and avocado pear: putting to sea at 0230 ensured I left the dinner behind in Freetown before going on watch!

Presumably for some good reason, of which the junior ranks again were unaware, we pressed on at 27 knots. The Canary Islands, the furthest north we had been for 19 months, were sighted looking lovely and the next day we swept into Gibraltar under a moonlit sky and secured alongside the oiler. There was a pencil of a searchlight steadily projected vertically into the sky for some obscure reason and lights all round the foot of the Rock.

Gibraltar for the Navy has the tradition of Piccadilly Circus: if you are there often enough you will meet all your naval friends. Sure enough when we were alongside next morning and I had forenoon watch on the quarterdeck, I saw a familiar figure coming along the mole - my brother Kenneth now a Sub-Lt. He had come in aboard the Black Swan Class sloop FLAMINGO having escorted a convoy on its way to Malta. After coming aboard and meeting my messmates in the wardroom we went off through the tunnel to Rosia Bay for a swim in the afternoon, then on to the Rock Hotel for dinner and a visit to FLAMINGO before he sailed at 2300 for Malta. A happy circumstance altogether which was to be repeated on several occasions throughout the war.

In the wardroom he had immediately been greeted as 'McSloth MkII' and this I must now explain. It was usual in a large wardroom such as ours for nicknames to be freely bestowed for any idiosyncrasy and 'Guns', 'Torps', 'Pig' and 'Tipsy' are a selection. On one occasion I had an argument with Geoffrey 'Torps' Carver, our delightful torpedo officer, over the pronunciation of the word 'sloth'. As I maintained the proper pronunciation was the Scottish way to rhyme with 'cloth' whereas he and the rest of the predominantly English officers insisted it rhymed with 'both'! No-one surrendered so consequently the name 'McSloth' stuck as long as I was in DORSETSHIRE and my lookalike brother was so greeted when he came aboard.

A significant purchase I made in Gibraltar was a pair of Zeiss 7x50 binoculars which must have been about the last pair on the Rock before supplies ran out. I had been conscious whilst keeping watch on the bridge for four hours at a time and observing the lookouts, whose alertness and concentration were the eyes of the ship before sophisticated radar and HF/DF[8] (Huff-Duff) became aids, that the good but heavy navy issue of Barr and Stroud binoculars inhibited the watchkeepers from holding the glasses to their eyes for any length of time. This may well have reduced the efficiency of the ship or for that matter the whole Navy by a factor of 10-20%. These German Zeiss binoculars were at least 20% lighter and better than the Barr and Stroud models - that is why I bought a pair and never regretted it. Later in the war in October 1943 I relieved Oberleutnant Spiedal of U-643 of his pair of Zeiss 7 x 50's after we had sunk his boat and eventually gave them to Kenneth. I told Spiedal who proved to be an unreconstructed, unpleasant Nazi, when we landed him and some of his crew at Greenock that he wouldn't be needing them where he was going.

On 22nd May, just as I was going for a dental appointment, we were placed on short notice and sailed at 1430 for Devonport amidst rising excitement throughout the ship. We sailed well out into the Atlantic before turning north and went into two watches i.e. four hours on and four

[8] High Frequency Direction Finding

32

hours off watch. This is a very tiring routine if kept up for long but we were now in active U-boat waters. During this time I was put through an examination by Brian Durant for my watchkeeping certificate which I passed but it still required the 'Owners' approval before being granted.

We reached Devonport on Saturday 25th May and anchored in the stream near Flagstaff Steps with the gentle UK rain drizzling down. Leave for a week was immediately given to half the ship as we were to be in port for only two weeks and I was granted the first week so in a flash I was over the side to telegraph Kirsteen at home. I made for the 4.15pm train to London which I missed, so took a taxi to Exeter and caught the connection there. After the usual packed and clattering night train I arrived in Glasgow at 9.10am to be met by Kirsteen who had taken 'compassionate' leave from the WAAF and Jimmy Dutton[9]. There was great joy all round at the station and we made for home and breakfast. An amazing week set in following the decision Kirsteen and I made to get spliced before I returned to the ship. Mrs Orr started organising a full scale white wedding by the Thursday. At the insistence of my father I shopped around and rented a flat, 73 Kelvin Court, which Kirsteen could have as her own home without being dependent on family or in-laws - what a very wise old man. We trawled round those who were on leave and had a party in the Piccadilly Club that evening – Willis Roxburgh was back from Iran and Cargill and Lyndsay Sandeman, my brother James and his wife Isobel, John Tindal and Meta and Nell Roxburgh, and others had fun. The following days were full rushing round lawyers, the office, and so on, but on the Wednesday, Willis and I took off to Troon for a round of golf in perfect weather. In between I saw as much as I could of my mother who was a great supporter of Kirsteen whom she had welcomed as the daughter she never had and had taken the trouble to get to know her whilst I was away.

The wedding was on the Thursday at 2.30pm in Westbourne Church taken by Kirsteen's uncle, the Reverend William Loudon, with the reception in the Central Hotel. During the reception a telegram from

---

[9] Kirsteen's sister, Jocelyn's husband-to-be

DORSETSHIRE was phoned in from my home ordering me back to the ship forthwith! Apparently one of the Lieutenants, Ian Cox, had been drafted to another ship and they were becoming short-handed. I took my time!

Glasgow Herald, 31ˢᵗ May 1940

> **MILLER-ORR.**- At Westbourne Church, Glasgow, on 30ᵗʰ May, 1940, by the Rev. William Loudon, Lieutenant Alan John McCulloch Miller, R.N.V.R., second son of Mr and Mrs Louis M. Miller, 3 Erskine Avenue, Glasgow, S.1, to Kirsteen Ross Orr, W.A.A.F., second daughter of Mr and Mrs Frank G. Orr, 5 Park Terrace, Ayr.

As can be imagined the wedding reception was on a high note - it was amazing the number of old friends who were still at home and had heard the news. Many came from the Army, which was still in training of course. Kirsteen's sister, Jocelyn, was the bridesmaid but in the awkward situation of having had her leave stopped, and I had to run down to the RAF base at Rhu to ask the CO if he would release her to attend the wedding. Apparently Jocelyn's boyfriend, the Norwegian pilot of a seaplane by which he had escaped from Norway, had given her some petrol for her car from his plane and both of them were duly arraigned! He agreed to release Jocelyn for the day on condition a couple of officers could accompany her to the wedding - I think they enjoyed it. Mr and Mrs Orr had done some amazing organisation in arranging such a wedding in four days. We caught the 6pm to Edinburgh, checked in at the North British Hotel (the NB) and dined and danced at the Caledonian Hotel's De Guise Restaurant.

Reluctantly responding to the summons from the ship - I had visions of her going off in support of the retreat to the sea of the Army in northern France - we therefore caught the 10am train for a slow journey to London. Booking into the Grosvenor House, we then headed for Hatchetts, that great wartime watering-hole, for dinner and a little dancing then on to the Cafe de Paris where Evelyn Laye was singing.

Mary Miller, the author's mother, and her brother, 'Uncle' John McCulloch, RNVR CO of ML 152 in the First World War.

Jimmy and Alan Miller -
Hunters Quay Summer 1917

Kelvinside Academy OTC Inspection, Summer 1930
Cadet Sgt Maj Jimmy Miller in command with Alan in the ranks: the sea rather than the kilt beckoned

Jimmy Miller, elder brother of the author.

Kenneth Miller, younger brother of the author, as a Midshipman RNVR in December 1939. Subsequently a qualified gunnery officer of the 'U' Class Fleet destroyers

By now we had stopped drinking champagne - until the next time. We had a stroll around Bond Street and Regent Street on Saturday morning coming down to earth and the realities of the Army's plight and the evacuation from Dunkirk. We caught the packed-like-sardines 1.15pm train from Paddington to Plymouth and checked in to the Royal Hotel. I then went down to the DORSETSHIRE together with Kirsteen to find what the fuss was about. It was, as expected, all due to Ian Cox having had a quick posting to destroyers: in fact the opportunity was taken to draft many of our experienced men to other ships in the rapidly expanding Fleet. Ian Cox was a Scot from Fife and after the war he proposed me for membership of the R & A. This departure allowed me to move to his better cabin on the ship!

Kirsteen and I had moved to the Grand Hotel where a number of other officers' wives were staying so she was not alone during the hours I had to be on duty on board. Several of my messmates stood in for me on many occasions so that we could be together and visit the surrounding countryside and beaches. There were a few parties on board and Kirsteen enjoyed meeting my messmates and to see for herself what naval life was like. At the age of 21 and very attractive she was most compatible with the Subs and Midshipmen in the Gunroom and they made a great fuss of her - at their parties she enjoyed seeing the reversed 'Royal' pictures on the bulkheads which exposed 'pin-ups' on the back, and our Chinese stewards' special and lethal 'blue' cocktails which were passed around. Incidentally these Chinese stewards and dhobi wallahs were a feature of all ships on the China fleet. They were Hong Kong Chinese who were carried on the ships books and looked after the Officers and Petty Officers Messes. Our Head Steward was Buck Wing and it was he who plied the blue, Chartreuse-based, cocktail which was renowned throughout the Fleet.

On this first visit to the UK either they, the Chinese, or the Admiralty decided the war, the food or the climate was a bit rough for them, so sadly they left us and were shipped home. Little did they know they were going straight into the impending clutches of the Japanese. We missed them - our laundry was never the same!

Fortunately Gieves had by now invented stiff white cardboard collars which lasted several days before being thrown away.

The days of this bizarre honeymoon were quickly running out and we were selfishly making the most of it - Kirsteen's leave from the WAAF had already expired and telephone calls were chasing her and being ignored. I was leaning heavily on the goodwill, generously given, of my messmates standing in for my duties. It was the first week of June and all around us on this South Coast was confusion and apprehension as the deliverance of the Army from Dunkirk and France continued. Day after day the scene from Plymouth Hoe was amazing. French troops rescued from the Pas de Calais and Norway had been put on special trains to Plymouth in the West Country and shipped on commandeered cross-channel ferries to be taken back to Brest and other Brittany ports. As they sailed down Plymouth Sound the troops were singing the 'Marseillaise' - in the quiet of the evening it was very moving. At the same time British and Canadian troops - the 51st Highland Division and the 1st Canadian Division - were still being sent to Normandy and the ships carrying these troops also set sail down the Sound. It was a costly and ill-judged sacrifice to end with the surrender by General Victor Fortune at St Valery.

It was on Tuesday 4th June in the aftermath of Dunkirk and the evacuation of our forces from Norway, that Churchill made his great speech in Parliament to declare *"We will fight them on the beaches, we shall fight them on the landing grounds, we shall fight in the fields and in the streets, we shall fight in the hills: we shall never surrender"* etc. What a strange and dramatic week in which to enjoy a honeymoon but we made the most of it, and I clearly remember being quite confident and rational in reassuring Kirsteen that we on our island could never be invaded successfully which was of course the issue in everyone's' mind at that time. Despite this conviction, the situation was extremely serious but the mood was in no way defeatist as it seemed to be with our French allies. This was a major topic of special interest amongst my naval colleagues as the fate and commitment of the French Navy, if France was overrun, was of vital importance to our immediate future.

Churchill, on 11th June, at his last of many meetings with the French Government and Chiefs of Staff on French soil at Briare near Orleans, had had a talk alone with Admiral Darlan, CinC of the French Navy. Darlan then promised he would never let the Germans take over the French Fleet, the fourth largest in the world with modern ships and equipment. He was later to declare to the assembled meeting that he would never surrender the French Navy to the enemy: in the last resort, he had said, he would send it to Canada; but in this he might be overruled by the French politicians. However, when Darlan became Minister of Marine, and a politician in the collaboratist Petain Government, he rejected his previous promises and assurances and endeavoured to retain the French Fleet under Vichy control. He did not entirely succeed.

Meanwhile the hours of our honeymoon were running out and our time together was eroded by the responsibilities I had on board DORSETSHIRE as we prepared to set off to sea again. On Saturday 8th June, Kirsteen came aboard at 1.30pm and saw my new cabin which I had inherited from Ian Cox enabling her to visualise where I was to live for the unforeseeable future.

Ashore she packed, and headed for the 4.15pm for London to find, not surprisingly in the prevailing chaos, that it wasn't running. So she caught a train via Bristol and began a horrendous journey to London for a night in the Euston Hotel then on up to Glasgow the next day to return to duty at MAEE at Rhu. Apparently her AWOL was forgiven!

Next day we sailed at 1500 to carry out de-gaussing[1] trials in Plymouth Sound then eventually sailed at midnight and set course 219° at 26 knots for Las Palmas in the neutral Canary Islands to try to intercept two Nazi merchantmen bottled up there since the outbreak of the war and now making a break for the west coast of occupied France.

At midnight on 10th June, Italy declared war which compounded our problems by lining up another large fleet against us and effectively closing the Mediterranean and Suez Canal to our merchantmen and

---

[1] Degaussing - demagnetize ship as precaution against magnetic mines with encircling current-carrying conductor

troop transports. Italian Somaliland would also have to be dealt with before our Red Sea access to the Middle East could be secured.

On 11th June we received a signal from the Admiralty to divert and seek out an Italian ship the FORTUNATA and then again at 1800 another cypher cancelled that. We were to join SHROPSHIRE and CUMBERLAND at a rendezvous with a convoy consisting of the QUEEN MARY, MAURITANIA, EMPRESS of BRITAIN, EMPRESS of CANADA, ANDES and AQUITANIA carrying Commonwealth troops to the UK. We met them at 1000 on the 12th and these huge liners in one convoy charging along at 22 knots presented an extraordinary sight - like the Manhattan skyline on the move. I had the first watch and later noted in my diary that *"I suffered rubber truncheon from the Owner on getting into night cruising position astern of the convoy. He was wild"*. However that was all to change.

In response to yet another diverting signal, at dawn, we left this huge convoy to join HMS HOOD and four destroyers heading for Gibraltar at $28\frac{1}{2}$ knots. We found them at 1000 while I had the forenoon watch (8-12). As I was handing over at noon I spotted an object on the horizon about 12 miles away. This extended horizon was possible as our height-of-eye on the open bridge was about 60 feet above the waterline. On the waterline the horizon is about $3\frac{1}{2}$ miles distance.

My new Zeiss 7 x 50 binoculars convinced me it was a U-boat's conning tower and I called the Captain and sounded the 'Alarm' for action stations. The Walrus aircraft was immediately manned and catapulted off inside 10 minutes dropping four bombs on the U-boat. This caused her to dive and the destroyers kept her down until the HOOD and ourselves had passed. We retrieved the Walrus and the crew reported an oil slick and estimated damage but with my later experience of how tough the U-boats were, I don't believe the small bombs carried by the Walrus would cause her mortal damage. Later in the day a passing Allied merchant ship signalled that a German raider was chasing her! We made her cancel her 'RRR' broadcast.

Altogether it was an exciting day so soon after getting back to sea, for me the happy outcome was that my stock had gone up in the

Captain's estimation and an RNVR might be of some use! The position of this incident was approximately 45° N 17° W.

By Saturday 15th June we had reduced speed to 22¹/₂ knots to reach Gibraltar by Sunday morning with the intent to oil and resume our foray to the Canaries in the event of Spain deciding to join the Axis Powers. That day the French Army surrendered so we were surrounded by enemies, potential enemies and defeated allies. We found ourselves in an apprehensive situation as Gibraltar could have been the first place to be attacked by Spain. As it was I had strawberries for tea and a swim at Rosia Beach.

And at last the Captain gave me my watchkeeping certificate for a major war vessel with a smile and a lecture - indirectly thanks to the Zeiss 7 x 50's!

On 10th June the British under General Fortune surrendered at St Valery and it didn't take Colonel Rommel, in command of the 7th Panzer Division, long to roll up 8000 men of the 51st Highland Division together with 400 Frenchmen and put them in the bag.

In the wake of the continued collapse of the French Army and the request of the Petain Government for an armistice on 17th June, the remains of our Army in France started to embark at Cherbourg and other French ports together with as much equipment as they could save. It was another Dunkirk but undertaken by larger vessels. In all 136,000 British troops and 20,000 Polish were evacuated. But there was a horrendous incident off St Nazaire when the hospital ship, SS LANCASTRIA, received a bomb directly down her funnel just as she was leaving and upwards of 3000 soldiers perished. This was kept from the British public at that time to avoid further damage to morale.

Chapter V

VICHY FRANCE AND DAKAR
June 1940

By 17th June 1940 it didn't seem as though Spain was going to join the Axis in this war or for that matter the Allies, so our particular problem, and it was on the doorstep, was the destiny of the powerful French Fleet. Away over our heads the political drama surrounding this issue was developing. Churchill was in the thick of it negotiating with Admiral Darlan who, on the morning after the French Government capitulated (17th June), had reassured Churchill that the French fleet would never fall into German hands. By the end of the month he had reneged on this commitment and, as his authority over the French Fleet was for all practical purposes absolute, the British Admiralty took independent action. All French ships in UK ports were taken firmly under British control on 3rd July but the ships overseas, principally at Oran in North Africa, had to be violently coerced by Admiral Somerville's Force 'H' from Gibraltar. On the 17th I had a pleasant dinner with my Clyde Division friend James Black on board HMS RESOLUTION one of Somerville's Force 'H' battleships standing by . He was to be in action in Oran a few days later. A day or two later the battleship HOOD and carrier ARK ROYAL arrived to reinforce the group. On the 23rd we left Gibraltar at 0600 for Dakar in French Senegal in driving rain and a strong west wind. With us was the destroyer HMS WATCHMAN who eventually left us for Casablanca to monitor any French warships lurking there, particularly the newly built battleship JEAN BART recently arrived from the builders yard at St Nazaire but as yet without her guns. She must be prevented from getting into enemy hands. The RICHELIEU, another powerful nearly new battleship, had reached Dakar with her 15" guns and control systems operational. This was our quarry which, hopefully through the French authorities ashore, had to be persuaded to come over to the Allies. Failing that she had to be put out of action for the future. If either of these modern battleships, which were fully mobile but had not yet completed their fitting out or trials, had been allowed to reach Toulon, the principal French naval base, comparable to Devonport or Portsmouth, they would have been potentially powerful additions to Axis naval strength. Approaching Dakar we flew off the Walrus to reconnoitre but unfortunately a wing was bent when hoisting her back on board subsequently restricting our shadowing capability.

On the 25th June we reached Dakar but the RICHELIEU had sailed shortly before. We endeavoured to intercept and shadow her but were of course handicapped, with our plane not yet being operational. We were dashing about the ocean at 30 knots with visibility closing in as a sandstorm filled in from the desert to the east. The Walrus was ready for service by dawn and was flown off at 0500. And now she was herself lost in this deteriorating condition and had to make a forced landing on the sea at 0830! We tried to D/F each other but to no avail. Miraculously she saw RICHELIEU heading south and gave us her course and speed enabling us to find and remain in shadowing contact until we saw she was returning to Dakar. Where she was heading for in the first place we never knew but the assumption was she intended to break back into the Mediterranean and Toulon to complete her fitting out. The confrontation at Oran on 3rd July had not yet taken place. We resumed our search for the Walrus and her crew into the 27th and were in contact by radio every hour but her batteries were getting weak and visibility was bad. Our old friend the aircraft carrier HERMES joined in the search with her planes and eventually gave us a lead enabling us to come on her with a quarter of a mile's visibility at 1000. There was a big cheer from the whole ships company as we hoisted 'Tipsy' Tarver, the pilot, and Harry Parker, the observer, aboard in the tough and faithful 'shagbat'. We turned again for Dakar with the Admiralty asking us how much fuel we had left! 50% was the answer.

On the 28th we made another stab at getting into Dakar but having established RICHELIEU was safely anchored in harbour with awnings spread we waited outside from 0500–1000 when we received a signal to head for Freetown *"with all dispatch"* (i.e. at 30 knots) which we made at dawn on the 29th and then oiled immediately. Our Captain went off to confer with the CinC, Admiral D'Oyle Lyon, for an update on the situation. Life was getting a bit hectic as we turned around at 1700 and headed back to Dakar! We met HERMES off Dakar on the 30th and took over surveillance of RICHELIEU from about 15 miles offshore closing in to 3 miles at night. She remained inside the harbour boom like an elegant City Chambers.

This patrolling went on for several days during which we were at 2nd degree Action Stations taking only a few minutes below for meals. I was sharing Air Defence Officer duties with Lt Harry Parker - very trying and boring. Aircraft from Dakar came over from time to time but stayed out of range. At 1600 on 4th July we spotted a French submarine surfacing to enter the harbour and catapulted the Walrus to go in and bomb her. She missed but our puny bombs probably wouldn't have done much harm anyway. At dawn on the 5th we were joined by HERMES and HMAS AUSTRALIA and at the same time orders were received that unless attacked we were only to observe and shadow RICHELIEU. Perhaps this reflected the outcome of Admiral Somerville's attack on the French fleet in Oran. On the 7th we were joined by the sloop HMS MILFORD which went into the harbour at 1400 to deliver an ultimatum to the Governor to surrender all French warships, including RICHELIEU of course, but she was told to scram or be shot up. Our ultimatum was to expire at 2000. Meanwhile the several Captains conferred aboard HERMES whose Capt Onslow had just been promoted to Rear-Admiral, much to the chagrin of our Capt Martin, and was therefore the Senior Officer of our little group.

The main thrust of the action to be taken, should the 2000 ultimatum expire without compliance by the French authorities ashore, was to neutralise the RICHELIEU. To this end volunteers were called for from the ships of our force to undertake a rather dicey mission and there was a good response. Each of the cruisers carried what was known as a 'skimmer', a 16 foot fast motor boat for use by the Captains to visit their chums on other ships in harbour.

The plan proposed by DORSETSHIRE was to balance two depth charges on the stern of the skimmer, set the fuses to 'shallow', then creep into the harbour and drop the charges under the stern of the RICHELIEU and explode them near her propellers. This was brilliantly carried out at 0300 by Lt Cdr 'Bobby' Bristowe RN of HERMES and this, co-ordinated with a torpedo attack by Swordfish aircraft from HERMES, resulted in a spectacular explosion. At daylight the RICHELIEU was seen to be settled by the stern. Our objective to immobilise the RICHELIEU was achieved and the skimmer was picked up unharmed off Dakar at noon. Some French planes came out in the forenoon and dropped a few bombs to no effect. This gave Parker and me the opportunity to open up our anti-aircraft Pom-Poms and Oerlikons - also to no effect! It all seemed very strange to be assaulting our ally of two weeks ago.

Although the damage inflicted on RICHELIEU achieved its objective, it did not prevent her taking a major part with her 15" guns in resisting a later attack on Dakar from 23rd-25th September headed by General Charles de Gaulle who was attempting to persuade the pro-Vichy authorities to come over to the Free French. The invasion did not succeed and some of our ships including the RESOLUTION were badly mauled: incidentally RICHELIEU was hit by one of her 15" shells and could now be definitely dismissed as a hostile factor in our calculations.

At night on 9th July HERMES and ourselves set off for Freetown zigzagging all the way. At 0300 in a wild rainstorm HERMES crashed into the AMC CORFU leading a convoy. CORFU was holed forward and HERMES bent badly and they remained locked together until daybreak when they managed to tear apart. In the confusion other ships of the convoy tried to ram us but all was well. A tug from Freetown took CORFU in tow and with us shepherding them we all headed there at 3 knots! We arrived on the 12th and spent a quiet four days in very wet and steamy conditions. Fortunately some mail arrived from home and I exchanged visits for dinner and a gossip with Bill McLachlan from Clyde Division who was in HERMES. On 17th July we set off on patrol to 35° W 20° N to try to intercept a 9000 ton commerce raider following reports of two British ships missing in that area. We cruised up and down on Latitude 30° W in the hope of an 'RRR' signal within striking distance. There was too much swell to operate the Walrus.

A signal came to intercept the Portuguese (neutral) SS COLONIAL, a passenger ship from Pernambuco and take off the Italian Consul. We flew off the 'shagbat' and spotted COLONIAL at 1300 near St Paul's Rock and then sent off a boarding party to take off the Consul, Signor Tranquillo Bianchi, on whom I practised my elementary German for many days. The AMC ALCANTARA had on 28th July met the raider we were looking for and came off second best being holed in the engine room while the raider, which was the THOR (Ship No 10, Raider 'E'), turned away after being hit herself, made smoke and sailed off to a quiet spot in the South Atlantic where she carried out her own repairs and replenished from a supply ship. ALCANTARA was able to put into Rio de Janiero for repairs.

We continued patrolling and searching, returning for a quick refuel to Freetown as there appeared to be a couple of raiders operating south of the equator. On the 31st there was a 'RRR' from the British ship DOMINGO DE LARRINGA being attacked about 600 miles south-west of our position. We reached the estimated area of attack at dawn on the 1st August but the bad weather we had had for nearly two weeks made it impossible for us to operate the Walrus thereby cutting down the effectiveness of our sweeps. During this month of July seven other ships had disappeared on the South American route, all but one destroyed by THOR. The strategy of CinC South Atlantic and his staff based in Freetown, poor souls, assessed that the enemy was unlikely to strike twice in the same area and kept DORSETSHIRE and CUMBERLAND patrolling the Cape route in the expectation the raiders would choose this area next. But this hope was not fulfilled.

However much fortune might favour an individual commerce raider, this policy of going where he was most likely to strike was the only one which eventually would produce results. The South Atlantic was too vast an area in which to act otherwise.

The boredom of endless days of patrolling up and down the trade route to the Cape with sorties to the South American coast was mitigated by sunny days, blue seas and starry nights. Off watch we read, played bridge but not poker, chess and the ubiquitous naval favourite 'ukkers', otherwise draughts. For exercise we walked back and forth on the teak laid quarter deck and occasionally played a violent version of deck hockey with a wooden puck. Freetown offered a golf course and good swimming beaches when we were in harbour. One diversion was an amusing sortie in the Walrus with the No 1, Paddy Boyle, and the pilot, 'Pig' Lucas, following the river up-country as far as Port Lokko and shooting at crocodiles with Tommy guns on the way! We crossed the equator so many times that it was no longer an event and as this was compounded by the navigator positioning us precisely on the equator when going east to west at about 16 knots and zigzagging every 20 minutes for 2 days that DORSETSHIRE should surely claim an entry in the Guinness Book of Records. When we were stooging about on the Tropic of Capricorn (20° S) on 5th August a raider was reported oiling from a supply ship about 30 miles off St Helena, so we buzzed up to 25 knots and reached St Helena at 0030 on the 6th when we hoisted out the Walrus and anchored in what passes for a harbour there. The pilot, Tarver, and observer had a couple of hours sleep then took off at dawn to flush out, what seemed to us on board, our best chance so far to make a kill. However there was no sign of any ship over a wide expanse of sea despite an all day patrol by the Walrus in perfect weather. We returned to Freetown without having seen one ship.

News from home was worrying with huge air battles being waged over the Channel as the Battle of Britain was reaching its height; the outcome for Britain as yet unknown.

Our next patrol took us back down to St Helena by 22nd August and this time we went in and anchored in Jamestown harbour, a picturesque old fashioned town with bumboats circling round selling lace, fruit and postcards of Napoleon's house.

The Walrus was sent off on a couple of observation sorties to justify our presence there and on the 25th we set off at dawn to rendezvous with the Dutch cruiser SUMATRA in the evening. The crew were manning the rails in straw hats and the officers were lined up on the quarter-deck. Our band played the Dutch national anthem and then she set off for Lobito handing over her charge, the liner ORION with 300 children on board, for us to escort to Cape Town. After a stormy passage we reached Table Bay on the 29th and then went round to Simons Town. A large convoy of small ships together with the ANDES and EMPRESS OF BRITAIN carrying troops were in False Bay sheltering from a gale. We had two anchors down and a bridge watch at the ready. This visit presaged another pleasant spell at the Cape. When we went alongside I phoned my contacts and arranged to see Ginger Brukman for a farewell evening before he joined up. Similarly Angus Duncan was in quarantine with the Cape Town Highlanders before heading for the Middle East. He was the CO. This didn't interfere with some golf at the Royal Cape with Lady Haggard and a Mrs Findlay.

Harry Parker became engaged to a very glamorous South African girl, Muriel Coram, whom he had met on our last visit so we had a party in the Bohemia Club to celebrate the occasion. The next day we were off up the coast to Durban having embarked a draft of RNVR's consisting of four sub-lieutenants and 84 ratings for training and subsequent service in the Royal Navy. A pleasant leavening to our predominately RN complement.

After a rough passage, which is the par for that coast, we reached Durban at dawn on 5th September and were in dock for a scrub and an attack on the defect list by the dockyard. Despite the security supposedly attached to our movements it was no surprise to us to find Muriel Coram and her mother on the quay at Durban, up from Cape Town to welcome her fiancé in. Perhaps because of my recent experience in these matters, Harry Parker had asked me to be best man at his wedding to Muriel in the next few days. A word about Harry: he was a qualified Fleet Air Arm pilot but had crashed so many planes he wasn't allowed to touch the Walrus but occasionally flew as an observer; his other notable feature was five initials, H.F.J.T.P.: perhaps his mother wasn't sure who his father was and decided to cover the options. In the absence of a support group of relations the office of Best Man turned out to be a comprehensive exercise away beyond getting Harry to the church on time and not to forget the ring. I had to organise the wedding in St. Paul's Cathedral, the Reception at the Durban Club afterwards - which boasts the longest bar south of the Equator - and details like the traditional garland to hoist on the triatic stay (wire between the masts) of DORSETSHIRE, the party of officers with an arch of swords at the church door, and the car pulled by sailors to take the happy pair to the reception. Harry was a popular officer and there was a tremendous turnout of the ships company at the service and no lack of volunteers to man the traces of the car through the streets of the Town.

The days in Durban were pleasantly spent although I found the hot and sticky climate uncomfortable. The golf course at the Country Club was superb; very like a links course in Scotland and there was a little golf course laid out inside the city's racecourse which was fun. Durban lived up to its marvellous reputation for entertaining visiting ships including the troop ships on their way to the Middle East war zone. There must be many sailors who have special memories of their touch-down there.

One of our officers, Lt Cdr Tom Fox-Pitt, was a 'dug-out' (a RN officer who had been retired in the Geddes Axe rundown of the Navy in the early 1930's and recalled for WWII) who had retired to South Africa with his wife Caroline and family and lived near Durban. She organised an exciting visit for a few of us to the Hluhluie Game Reserve about 185 miles north of Durban. After an excellent lunch in the Edward Hotel to fortify us we set off at 2 o'clock on 14th September north to Tongaat, over the Tugela Bridge to Empangeni, Mtubatuba and the Reserve which we reached at half-past midnight. The roads were single track and very rough; the 'rondavaals' were also pretty basic but we were up at 5.30 am and off with a Zulu guide to see the fantastic wildlife on offer; the Reserve supported every imaginable animal except elephant but included the, even then, rare White Rhino. To me the exotic bird-life was particularly surprising and fascinating. We were back on board by the 17th when the Wardroom Mess formally dined on board in Mess Kit for the first time since the war had broken out.

At 0700 the next morning we left for Simons Town, crashing into huge seas and storm force winds; it was the worst weather I had yet experienced and I came off watch covered in salt from the spray drenching us at 60 feet above the sea. At one time we had to reduce speed to 8 knots to avoid damage. However this was compensated by a lovely batch of mail when we arrived alongside. This comment in my diary prompts me to give my opinion of where on the oceans the worst weather is to be experienced and expected: by this I mean not just the occasional hurricane or typhoon, which usually occurs in normally calm areas, but more or less constant heavy seas. This area off Cape Agulhas at the southernmost point of Africa, where the cold Atlantic current flows into the warm Indian Ocean over a relatively shallow shelf and is driven by unobstructed winds from the South Atlantic, offers the biggest seas and, incidentally, the largest concentration of marine wrecks anywhere, including the notorious HMS BIRKENHEAD[10] famed for the original 'women and children first' discipline. Whilst Cape Horn seems to suffer from the most persistent and strong winds, in my experience the most unpleasant stretch of water in the world is the Arctic Ocean and the Barents Sea. Here you have again a relatively shallow area constantly whipped up by the prevailing south-westerlies generating very steep short seas making life on board any vessel extremely uncomfortable. Given a change of wind to the north or east the temperature drops to freezing and life on board is hell.

Returning to my story, I did a bit of phoning around but everyone seemed to be out of town or had gone off to the war; Angus Duncan

---

[10] The Troopship BIRKENHEAD, an iron paddle steamer of 1400tons and 556 hp commanded by Master Commander Robert Salmond, sailed from Cork on 7th January 1852 with 631 persons aboard bound for the Cape. Included in her number was a draft from the 91st (Argyllshire) Highlanders. At 0200 on 26th February the ship struck a jagged rock off Simons Town. Not a women or child perished but 438 souls were drowned, mostly soldiers that had stood to attention on the deck as the BIRKENHEAD broke her back and slipped between the waves. The rocks she struck are now known as the Birkenhead Rocks. *See* The History of the 91st Argyllshire Highlanders, *pp 152-154*, by R P Dunn-Pattison, *William Blackwood and Sons 1910*.

was with his regiment in Pretoria and Francis with her family at Hermanus. From her I learned that Willis Roxburgh had arrived in the troopship STIRLING CASTLE and after visiting her had gone off to Rhodesia to learn to fly at one of the Empire training schools there.

We turned around quickly and left Simons Town at 1400 on the 21st for the now familiar delights of Freetown. The big bombardment of the Vichy dominated French Fleet at Dakar, reinforced by three cruisers from Toulon, which had slipped past Gibraltar due to a cock-up at the Admiralty, had started but we were too late to take part. We also heard on the radio that Glasgow had been bombed on the 23rd September which was disturbing.

Our course was now towards Ascension Island in the never ending search for the commerce raiders; at this time the THOR was back in business after her brush with the AMC[11] ALCANTARA at the end of July. The Dakar confrontation was still going on and our companion ship CUMBERLAND had been hit and was now in Bathurst licking her wounds.

We closed in to half a mile off Ascension on the 26th which looked a pretty barren sort of place not unlike Tristan da Cunha. Eventually we pitched up in Freetown on the 29th where the harbour was full of warships from the Dakar debacle; some of them badly damaged with HMS RESOLUTION the worst hit having been torpedoed and showing a marked list.

There now follows a brief explanation of the references in my diary to Dakar and this little known episode in the chaotic consequences of the fall of France. The War Cabinet was greatly concerned that Germany would coerce Vichy France into conceding France's West African territories as part of an armistice deal enabling U-boat bases supported by German aircraft to be set up all down the African coast.

The spearhead of the initiative to frustrate this possibility was to be General de Gaulle and his Free French forces made up of two battalions, some tanks, guns and aircraft together with whatever French warships could be persuaded to participate to add to our ships. This

---

[11] Armed Merchant Cruiser

invasion force was assembled in Liverpool in mid-August and scheduled to refuel in Freetown for a landing at Dakar on 18th September. Security for the operation was lax and in Liverpool it was common knowledge amongst the French troops gathered there that they were heading for a landing at Dakar. Probably as a consequence three French cruisers of the Georges Leygues Class, accompanied by three destroyers, left Toulon on 10th September and passed through the Straits of Gibraltar at full speed at 0830 on 11th September. As mentioned earlier, but for a fatal delay in signals reaching the First Sea Lord from the Foreign Office and the Director of Operations Force 'H' at Gibraltar under Admiral Somerville, the Navy would have been able to intercept them. As it was, the French cruisers sped south and reached Dakar unmolested. The naval escort of the invasion force, now south of Dakar on their way to Freetown to refuel, was signalled early on 14th September to break off and divert to Dakar to prevent the French cruisers entering. When this force consisting of the ARK ROYAL, CUMBERLAND, DEVONSHIRE and AUSTRALIA reached Dakar late on the 14th the French squadron was already in harbour with awnings spread. Meanwhile we were in dock at Durban.

This chapter of accidents sealed the fate of the Franco-British expedition to Dakar, although it was decided, under pressure from De Gaulle to negotiate with the Vichy Governor ashore to persuade them to join the Free French. De Gaulle's envoys landed from two aeroplanes on the local Dakar airfield under the Tricolour and a white flag and were arrested.

The fleet closed in to within five thousand yards and were immediately fired on by a shore battery hitting the destroyer INGLEFIELD and initiating a general engagement. The weather was foggy which added to the confusion. HMS CUMBERLAND was badly damaged and had to withdraw. Although the RICHELIEU had been disabled during our previous confrontation in early July, she was capable of firing two-gun salvos from her 15" turrets which influenced Admiral Cunningham. In the afternoon of the 15th De Gaulle tried to land his troops outside the town but had to withdraw. The action was resumed over the next two days at ranges of up to twenty one thousand yards (12 miles), in the face of heavy and accurate fire from the shore batteries and ships in harbour. RICHELIEU was targeted by the battleships BARHAM and RESOLUTION but continued firing. Eventually RESOLUTION was torpedoed by a Vichy submarine and put out of action for many months.

Although the operation could not be claimed as a success it did prevent the spread of Vichy influence to the garrisons in French Equatorial Africa and within a fortnight De Gaulle had established himself at Douala in the Cameroons which became a rallying point for the Free French cause. It also enabled the Allies to develop and keep open the Trans-Atlantic air transport route from the United States to Takoradi and the Middle East.

In DORSETSHIRE we returned to Freetown on 29th September to find the harbour full of the Dakar invasion squadron licking its wounds; RESOLUTION and CUMBERLAND being the worst hit. The bad news was that 'Tipsy' Tarver, our pilot who had been transferred to ARK ROYAL, had been shot down and killed in the attack on Dakar. I went over to RESOLUTION to commiserate with Jimmy Black who was a bit 'sore-stricken' and not looking forward to the lengthy refit in prospect. After an initial patch up in Simons Town she went to the United States for a full repair, which had its compensations.

We spent the next couple of weeks in Freetown going in and out to exercise the armament and that dreadful device known as the paravane. This was developed in the 1914 -1918 War to protect cruisers and larger ships from mines and torpedoes. It consisted of permanently fitted booms with cutters attached along the hull above the waterline, which were then swung out, to sever the mine moorings so rendering the mines inert. This exercise was hilarious with lots of shouting and cursing - one was fortunate to have a station well away from the bridge and the Captain when the paravanes were being streamed. In my opinion they were a useless device, reducing the speed and manoeuvrability of the ship in action.

Having embarked an armed guard of Royal Marines under

command of Lt Seth-Smith and Sub Lt Fox, we set sail for Takoradi on the Gold Coast to sequester a Vichy French ship, the TOUAREG. On arrival on 10th October we put the guard aboard and sailed in company for Keta where we put the bolshy Vichy French members of TOUAREG's crew ashore to walk back to France or wherever. We sailed on with the TOUAREG, eventually handing her over to HMS DELHI to take on to Douala further east along the Bight of Benin in the Cameroons. Off we went to the west at 23 knots on a long shot search for a reported raider and crossed the equator yet again on a course towards St Paul's Rocks and Pernambuco in Brazil. With no sign of the enemy we turned again for Freetown on the 15th but were diverted on the 17th to try to intercept Vichy French cruisers heading south. Despite flying off Walrus patrols we couldn't find them so eventually retired to the pleasures of Freetown and the consolation of a mail bag from home. There was a huge convoy of troop ships in harbour on their way to the Middle East. The vessels of the convoy were the ORONTES, MONARCH of BERMUDA, GEORGIC, DUCHESS OF YORK, CAPE TOWN CASTLE and WINCHESTER CASTLE carrying 15,000 troops. The next day we were off at 0700 to escort this convoy at 18 knots to Cape Town. It proved an easy and pleasant passage although station keeping when on watch, especially at night with all ships blacked out and the whole fleet zigzagging, was exacting. One of the watchkeepers, Lt Cheeke (replacement pilot for Tipsy Tarver) lost the convoy three times on the passage and nearly came close to being banished to the Crow's Nest! We peeled off the escort as we approached the Cape and went alongside in Simons Town at 1230 on the 28th October. That evening Officers from the troopships, which included some of the 51st Highland Division, were entertained to a party and dance at the Kelvin Club in Cape Town to which myself and other DORSETSHIRE officers were invited. There I met lots of old friends from Scotland: Ian McLintock (who at this time of writing is in Erskine Hospital), George Gardiner, John Shields and Bill McLachlan to name a few and we had a great night together. I'm afraid I broke leave returning back to the ship at 0445 in the old De Soto. However by afternoon I was off again, this time to the Royal Cape Golf Course for a game with Bill McLachlan.

Next day we left with our convoy to round the Cape and headed north to Madagascar and the Red Sea. On board there was a small drama: 'Uncle Tom' Cobley, a dug-out Lt Cdr, who had been with us since Devonport had been hitting the bottle resulting in the Captain monitoring his messbill every month. There was talk of other behavioural backslidings all of which resulted in him being put ashore at Simons Town and he was replaced by an experienced South African RNVR, Lt Berlyn, who proved to be a real asset to the mess. This episode was a replica of what happened to Lt Cdr Paddy Boyle when we were in Devonport in May: in his cups[12] there he told the Captain what he thought of him and we didn't see him thereafter. He was a splendid shipmate.

For some reason not known to us the convoy we were escorting was reduced to the ORONTES, MONARCH of BERMUDA, DUCHESS OF YORK and the GEORGIC but when we were off the south end of Madagascar we joined a slower convoy going north at 14 knots also carrying troops of the 51st Highland Division. Two of the ships, K.I. CAUTH and the ERIN, peeled off to Mombasa.

We were now at permanent anti-aircraft stations in daylight hours as we were within range of the enemy in Italian Somaliland. On 8th November we crossed the Equator yet again. I had been drafted to the Commanders office which was most instructive and a step up in my naval learning curve as I was in charge of the plot and the signal traffic. To augment this I asked Capt Martin if I could have the ships 'Fighting Instructions' to study. Initially he refused on the grounds that I was an RNVR and a potential security risk! After twelve months at sea under his command it was a dreadful insult and when I told John Westmacott, the Commander, of this rebuttal he remonstrated with Martin and I gained access to the book. Before I simmered down I had mentally written several *"I have the honour to be"* letters to the CinC!

---

[12] A little worse for ware and full of Dutch courage.

Continuing into the Red Sea, with the weather getting hotter and hotter, we were given a couple of anti-submarine frigates to sweep ahead of us and the convoy, as well as a standing patrol by a Blenheim bomber. We passed Aden at noon on 12th November and assumed 2nd degree of readiness (i.e. watch on, watch off) at 2000 on the 13th when we were opposite Massawa where there were seven Italian destroyers, three submarines and three E-boats in the harbour.

I kept a seven hour watch with Lt Cheeke during the night of the 13th. My eyes were popping when I went below. The Iteyes had a wonderful opportunity for a torpedo attack on the convoy in the moonlight of that night. We left the convoy at 0930 on the 14th to go on its way to the desert battlefields of North Africa and, turning back through the columns of ships, we cleared lower deck and gave the troops a great cheer as we passed through. I sent a good luck signal to Ian McLintock on the MONARCH OF BERMUDA as we passed on opposite courses and received a nice reply.

Zigzagging at 21 knots we reached Aden at noon on the 15th and after oiling I had a run ashore with David Youatt, an RNVR engineer officer. A walk and drinks at the Union Club was followed by dinner at the Crescent Hotel.

I immediately contacted the sloop, HMS FLAMINGO, which was in harbour as I had learnt from my brother Kenneth's letter received in Freetown four weeks before that he was on board. Most disappointingly the reply was that he had transferred to another ship, HMS HUNTLY, a coal-burning ex-minesweeper, three weeks previously and was now again in the Mediterranean.

It was during this visit to Aden that we were fitted with an aircraft warning radar – the first radar any of us had been 'ship-mates' with. The whole apparatus together with operators had been flown out from the UK and its ability to pick up aircraft at 30 to 40 miles, depicted on a rather fuzzy screen, was magical. From then on the war at sea and the effectiveness of the Navy advanced in one huge leap.

We left Aden on 17th November and sailed south for Durban but on the way had a little business to attend to. On the very tip of the Horn of Africa is the port of Dante inside Ras Hafun in Italian Somaliland which had substantial naval installations such as oil tanks and piers with cranes. At 1400, donning our No 10's with long trousers, etc, and the sailors in long duck trousers as anti-flash protection, hoisting our battle ensigns for the first time and streaming the dreaded paravane contraptions, we opened fire. The Walrus had been catapulted off to act as a spotting plane and drop her bombs on the oil tanks. There was no reply from any shore batteries as it was probably siesta time but the Walrus received some light machine gun fire and was holed five times.

Natal Mercury, 30ᵗʰ November 1940

RAS HAFUN SHELLED

London, Friday. – Ras Hafun, near Cape Guardafui in Italian Somaliland has been successfully bombarded by a British ship with aircraft co-operation, says an Admiralty announcement made in London tonight. Two large fires were started and considerable damage done to enemy depots. The British forces suffered no casualties. SAPSA-Reuter.

We opened fire from our 8" guns targeting the port installations until the whole area was a cloud of black smoke. This was the first time I actually saw shells flying through the air. The 4" anti-aircraft guns then got their chance when we were closer and I engaged a hangar and the pier house. Finally our torpedo officer Geoffrey Carver had his chance when the Captain said *"Wouldn't it be fun to send in a torpedo"* and so with his fingers crossed he launched one set at shallow at the piers and there was a very satisfying explosion on the target. We had fired two hundred 8" shells, one hundred and forty 4" shells, one torpedo and several bombs from the Walrus which had been recovered and sent in again with another load. Fire had been opened at 14,000 yards closing to 4,000 when the torpedo was fired. Our damage was the loss of one awkward paravane. There was a second column of dust behind the town and this we identified as the Arabs and Iteyes heading for the hills.

We resumed our southerly course across the equator once again and through the Mozambique Channel to Durban in no great hurry with the only excitement being the theft of gin from the Gunroom which resulted in a fruitless (or should I say ginless) search of the ship and presumably some happy sailors. By the 26th November we were alongside in Durban and activated our hospitable contacts there with some golf at the splendid Country Club course as well as the funny little course in the centre of the race course. I can't leave Durban without recalling parties at the renowned Cosmo Night Club where the 'in' drink was brandy (excellent South African stuff) and milk! Medically it was probably very sustaining, depending on the dose.

We topped up our magazines with shells and one torpedo, sent up from Simons Town, after the splash at Dante. Eventually we left on 3rd December for Simons Town itself; that evening there was a loud crack from below so we slowed and trailed one propeller until we were able to go into dock to have it examined. Nothing wrong was found nor any evidence of having hit any underwater object so it remained a mystery.

After the usual delightful few days in Cape Town where a goodly batch of mail was awaiting us we were off again on the 10th October to pay penance for them in Freetown. I had asked the Captain if he would request some leave for me and he did write our CinC, Admiral Sir D'Oyle-Lyon, also suggesting I might now be sufficiently well trained for service in destroyers. Following implementation of the arrangement with the US Government of 50 old destroyers from their Reserve fleet and the increased output of destroyers from the UK shipyards there was a need for officers and men to man them and my 'vintage' of officers who now had over a year's sea experience could meet this bill.

Although commerce raiders with their supporting supply ships stationed in their rendezvous areas were reaching the high noon of their effectiveness, we in DORSETSHIRE seemed to have been left alone for the moment and there were no signals diverting us hither or thither for some weeks. So we reached Freetown at 0830 on 18th December and the Captain went for a meeting with the CinC. He sent for me when he returned and told me to pack for some leave in the UK and an appointment to a 'small ship' had been recommended. For the moment this move was dashed as an 'RRR' had been received and we were off at 1400 through the boom at 30 knots in company with the cruiser NEPTUNE heading due west to a sinking 800 miles away.

It was known that the ADMIRAL SCHEER had sailed from Stavanger on 28th October and the ADMIRAL HIPPER had passed through the Denmark Straits on 7th December so this incident was possibly a warship rather than a commerce raider. Post-war records based on information confirmed by our agents in Norway indicated that the SCHEER had in fact captured the British refrigerated vessel DUQUESA on the 18th whilst on the Freetown - South American route.

However, despite making 30 knots all the way and flying off the Walrus to reconnoitre, the ocean was empty of ships as far west as the islands of Fernando Novonha off the Brazilian coast. The SCHEER had quickly made off south to meet up with the raider THOR at their rendezvous area 600 miles north of Tristan da Cunha and hand over the captured DUQUESA to their supply ships cruising there.

It would have been a great coup albeit an almighty battle, with the battle cruiser having a fighting advantage, had we intercepted SCHEER on this occasion. She went on to inflict enormous damage sinking ten merchant vessels in the South Atlantic and Indian Ocean before returning to Bergen at the end of March 1941.

We flew off the Walrus every day in the hope of spotting the SCHEER and made a deep sweep to the south of the Equator, from time-to-time exercising tactics with NEPTUNE based on the GRAF SPEE experience. Eventually we were back across the Equator on Christmas Day and 500 miles from Freetown. After church with the off-duty watch for the first time we played a non-stop poker game aboard followed by a concert in the evening. Kirsteen had sent me a Christmas cake (unlikely to be home-made!) and I raffled it in the forward messes which was my Division. This made for quite a fun day especially as we were heading for Freetown; somewhere I never thought I would ever look forward to.

On arrival with NEPTUNE at 1300 on Boxing Day my discharge papers came aboard and having already packed my gear in anticipation I threw a few parties; one non-stop in the Wardroom, which Capt B C S Martin attended where he made a gracious little speech, then in between, one in the Gunroom and another in the Warrant Officers Mess to say thank you to these men who really ran the Navy and who helped me through many an awkward situation.

Just in case another 'RRR' signal sent us off again through the boom I didn't hang around and transferred to the depot ship EDINBURGH CASTLE where my farewell party continued with my particular chums from DORSETSHIRE. I had judged my departure perfectly as when I awoke the next morning DORSETSHIRE had sailed. It was bliss not being roused for the dawn action stations which was a painful discipline when at sea throughout the war. Even if you had turned in at 4am at the end of the middle watch you had to turn to for that critical period, especially in the tropics, when daylight flooded quickly over the sea and darkened ships, friendly or foe, were revealed. I determined that after the war I never wanted to see another dawn.

Next day, the 28th December, came a signal from CinC's office informing me to prepare for passage to the UK on the ORONTES returning from trooping to the Middle East where we had escorted her to in October. I was on board by 1300, settling in to a First Class cabin, with fresh linen, a comfortable bunk and a steward to bring morning tea - bliss. The ship was of course almost empty with only a draft of Australian naval ratings to disturb the peace. Vice Admiral John Cunningham, newly promoted 4th Sea Lord, who had flown his flag in NEPTUNE and been in charge of the Dakar fracas, was on board with his staff which made for pleasant company. For duties we organised the naval officers and ratings into U-boat look-out watches which required one watch a daylight day for me. Hogmanay passed quietly sobered by the awful news of a 500 plane, 10,000 incendiary bomb raid on London.

The days of the voyage passed in relaxed and comfortable idleness, reading and now sleeping with a couple of blankets for the first time since the winter of 1938-39. We stood well out into the Atlantic 30° W to avoid U-boats. My impatience now to get home was given a lift when a signal arrived changing our destination from Liverpool to the Clyde probably saving a couple of precious days in reaching home. On 9th January 1941 I woke to a lovely morning off the north-west coast of Ireland with Jura and Islay to port. After stopping at Rothesay boom control we anchored at the Tail of the Bank. I talked myself onto the Admiral's barge and landed at Princes Pier with all my luggage - camphor wood chests, golf clubs and all and was home at 73 Kelvin Court by 10pm.

And so now I relaxed for an indefinite spell of leave and a taste of married life without the mechanical crackle of the Tannoy SRE[13] dominating one's life.

Before signing off this chapter of my sixteen months in DORSETSHIRE I want to record highlights of the remainder of her career before she was eventually sunk by the Japanese. Still based in Freetown she continued to patrol the 'Atlantic Narrows' as we called it; that 1800 miles of ocean that lay between Africa and South America. She hunted the surface raiders as well as being a convoy escort to the increasing traffic of troop ships to and from the Middle East. The commerce raiders, especially the pocket battleships GRAF SPEE, ADMIRAL SHEER and DEUTSCHLAND, were outstandingly suitable as a weapon to employ against shipping lanes. With their diesel engines they had a huge cruising range and a high cruising speed of 26 knots maximum. Their objective was *"the continuous, ceaseless unease and disturbance to English trade"* rather than the number of ships they captured or sunk. Their instructions from the SKL were to *"avoid full engagement"* with the enemy but to strike at Allied merchant ships. If

---

[13] Sound reproduction equipment

the victim had managed to transmit an 'RRR', they were to make off immediately to the empty wastes of the ocean or a rendezvous with a supply ship to transfer her prisoners.

The disguised commerce raiders were controlled by similar instructions and they always made off as soon as they had made a conquest. Interestingly, DORSETSHIRE, with Capt A W S Agar VC now in command, had her only success in this long campaign on 1st December 1941, long after I had left the ship, when she caught the supply ship PYTHON fuelling and replenishing four U-boats 750 miles south of St. Helena. PYTHON was engaged in the clumsy task of transferring torpedoes to U-68. DORSETSHIRE's Walrus had spotted PYTHON at about 18 miles distance and, with evidence of U-boats in the vicinity, she fired two warning shots at 24,000 yards. PYTHON stopped her activities and began lowering boats and abandoning ship but DORSETSHIRE continued to zigzag at high speed and approached no nearer than 6000 yards. A third sortie by the Walrus confirmed that the PYTHON had sunk and 414 men were distributed in the motor-launches, ten rubber dinghies and the U-boats UA and U-68 took on board 100 men each. Other U-boats were ordered by SKL to take the crew and prisoners from PYTHON on board and after a saga of adventures involving four Italian submarines all arrived safely at St Nazaire.

As previously mentioned the ADMIRAL SCHEER was again loose in the southern oceans and following our 'near miss' off the South American coast around Christmas 1940, the SCHEER made for the Indian Ocean: sinkings north of Madagascar in February confirmed this. DORSETSHIRE was sent round the Cape to reinforce the hunting group tracking her down. During one of the aircraft searches, the Walrus crashed killing all the brave and dedicated crew who had recently been awarded the DSC, DSM and a Mention-in-Dispatches following the sinking of the BISMARCK. This was keenly felt by all on board.

The SCHEER was nearly caught by HMS GLASGOW whose Walrus sighted her on 22nd February about 100 miles north of Madagascar but she slipped away and presumably, having decided the

Indian Ocean was becoming too dangerous, returned to the South Atlantic and eventually back to Bergen on 30 March 1941. During this voyage she had sunk sixteen merchant ships totalling 100,000 tons and disposed of the AMC JERVIS BAY. Unfortunately GLASGOW, following temporary repairs, could do only 24 knots, with one turret and one propeller out of action after being hit by two aerial torpedoes at Suda Bay, Crete in December 1940. My good friend Cargill Sandeman, who joined the Clyde Division RNVR at the same time as I did, was in GLASGOW. He was Officer of the Watch when their Walrus returned to report it had sighted the SCHEER on the same course 90 miles ahead. Cargill recalls that when the Walrus signalled *"One pocket-battleship bearing ......, 90 miles"* he started to giggle with nervous excitement bringing down the wrath of the captain who furiously asked him *"what the hell are you laughing about?"* He replied it was the *"one"* he found droll.

After the sinking of HMS HOOD on 24th May 1941 by the BISMARCK and PRINCE EUGEN, a terrible blow to the Royal Navy, all available ships in the area were concentrated on hunting down the BISMARCK before she could reach Brest. She was eventually crippled and slowed down by aircraft from the ARK ROYAL. DORSETSHIRE had already detached herself from a convoy 600 miles to the south and arrived on the scene in time to pour 200 eight-inch shells into the BISMARCK and delivered the coup-de-grace with two torpedoes. Geoffrey Carver, 'Torps', must have been greatly content. She rescued 80 survivors despite a gale and heavy seas.

Finally, following the swift and deadly advance of the Japanese fleet to the westward in early 1942, DORSETSHIRE had reinforced the Eastern Fleet in the Indian Ocean under the command of Vice Admiral Sir James Somerville. First of all she helped to protect the last convoys from Singapore and Rangoon. On the approach of Admiral Naguno's fleet, Somerville cleared the harbours of Ceylon of ships but the Japanese carriers, in addition to sinking many merchant ships, caught DORSETSHIRE and CORNWALL about 400 miles south of Colombo and sank them both with the loss of 424 lives. HMS ENTERPRISE and two destroyers picked up 1,122 survivors; 19 officers and 215 ratings, many of them good mess mates of mine, were lost from DORSETSHIRE. As happens in these circumstances the burden of losses was in the engine room personnel and Cdr(E) Buttar, the Senior Engineer, Lt Cdr(E) Mansell, and Lts(E) Hooker and Wilson were lost as well as Surg-Cdr Bamford, our genial 'Doc'.

Admiral Somerville and Admiral Sir Geoffrey Layton, CinC Ceylon, did a tremendous job evacuating shipping from the harbours of Ceylon, thereby avoiding another Pearl Harbour, and although Admiral Nagano's Japanese carrier force did huge damage including the sinking of our chummy ship, the old carrier HERMES, his drive to the west expired that 5th/6th April 1942 ensuring our vital supply route round the Cape to the Middle East was not severed.

Japanese submarines did penetrate to the west coast of India, Madagascar and the East coast of South Africa with considerable success but Japan had too much on its plate contending with the Americans in the Far East to give them much support. However German U-boats and Italian submarines stepped up their penetration of the South Atlantic but that is another story in which I wasn't involved.

While DORSETSHIRE in my experience qualified as a happy ship, a difficult to define condition, it did not seem to yield the supply of senior officers for the Service which its complement of highly trained regulars would suggest. To my knowledge apart from Capt B C S Martin, who was promoted Rear-Admiral after the BISMARCK action, only one officer, Lt Brian Durant, subsequently reached Flag rank. I ascribe this to the overbearing and critical character of Martin who browbeat his officers and denigrated their capabilities. His 'Flimsy' S206s, reports on officers, must have made depressing reading.

Chapter VI

HMS BROCKLESBY
January 1941 – 7 November 1942

T he return home to our own apartment, 73 Kelvin Court, Kelvinside with no immediate naval appointment in view was a very happy time. Kirsteen was able to resign from the WAAF without much fuss as she had volunteered and joined before war broke out and compulsory service was not yet in force. She had taken on other voluntary commitments with a canteen for servicemen in Glasgow.

On another front Uncle John McCulloch had just died and left me the business of A & J McCulloch so it was opportune that I was around. This spell of leave enabled me to make arrangements with brother James and my father-in-law Frank Orr for the ongoing management of the business until I returned from the war. Both my parents were around and active and in particular my mother and Kirsteen had hit it off which to me was an especially welcome relationship at this time.

The days in my war diary turned over with no entries for many days and eventually weeks, but the time passed pleasantly including a visit to London with Kirsteen - sharing the only available sleeper bunk - where I risked a visit to Queen Anne's Mansions where RNVR officer appointments were determined. There I met Cdr Dennys for the first time who became a trusted contact in the years ahead. Apart from some happy evenings at the Cabaret Club renowned for its black painted walls and favoured by naval officers on leave, I made some business visits to ensure I hadn't been forgotten and let them know of the changes in the firm and the interim arrangements during my absence.

On the way north we stopped off for a few days in Birmingham which had recently been heavily bombed by the Luftwaffe and the damage was frightening. On top of this it was bitterly cold and snowing heavily. Another more pleasant trip at the beginning of February was to the north to visit friends billeted in Perth and Blairgowrie and meet up with Ralph and Sheena Dundas and George Crearar who were training in Army camps in that area. The sunny weather was just perfect.

Sorting out the business and arranging a management structure in the face of the call-up of staff was proving difficult and I asked the Admiralty for an extension of leave which was duly granted; proving both useful and enjoyable! This leave expired on 25th February but the days passed with no appointment. There was a launch of the corvette WOODROUGH at William Simons & Co Ltd where I was a non-executive director before becoming Chairman and Managing Director after the war, and the wedding of Willis' sister, Nell Roxburgh to Alan Fyfe on 6th March. Alan, who had a brilliant career ahead of him having been President of the Oxford Union, had joined the Argylls but sadly was killed in France with the 51st Highland Division on 7th August 1944 during the battle of the Falaise Gap.

The Navy caught up with me and off I went to Liverpool for an anti-submarine course at Western Approaches Command. I returned to Glasgow just in time to coincide with the greatest air raid of the war on the West of Scotland. It was the nights of the 13th and 14th of March. Kirsteen's sister, Jeanette, who was in the WAAF serving in the control tower at Prestwick airport had come up to Kelvin Court for the night and the three of us had been to hear 'Hutch', the jazz pianist, at the Empire Theatre then on to Rogano's for dinner. The anti-aircraft gunfire started about 9pm and then the bombs added to the horrific noise. We headed for home and the air raid shelter - on the way picking up a terrified young soldier to deliver him to Maryhill Barracks; he was more apprehensive at possibly overstaying his leave than being hit by a bomb.

This, the first heavy blitz on the west of Scotland by 250 bombers from Germany, Holland and Norway, did enormous damage to shipyards and munitions works such as the Singer munitions factory and the Rolls Royce engine works. It was repeated the following night by 300 bombers, with the previous night's fires still lighting up the whole riverside and surrounding country. Altogether about 700 people were killed and 2000 badly injured. The best description of this first big raid is given in a book I have 'Time of Crisis' by Andrew Jeffrey. Our flat in

Kelvin Court was not directly hit but most of the windows were blown in by the blasts which killed most of the resident population of mice that had previously enjoyed a comfortable centrally-heated existence. Having a car available we were able during the awful days that followed to assist the emergency services in ferrying people to hospital.

Towards the end of March I had a call from my appointer, McDougall, at the Admiralty to pack my bags quickly and go through to Perth Station the following night. This as usual was duly cancelled and I never heard what the panic was all about. Time rolled on pleasantly with the only major event being the purchase of the house, 9 Arnwood Drive, W2 not far from Kelvin Court on 10th May.

It was not until 23rd May 1941 that the telegram arrived to report to FOIC[14] Milford Haven by the 26th. I then had a spin round the family with a dinner of Millers and Orrs at the Marine Hotel, Troon. On the way home our Wolesey 10, CUS 161, ran a big end which rather slowed down my departure. However I caught the 5.40pm for Crewe experiencing the first of many sojourns at that gloomy junction. I rejected the train some time the next day at Carmarthen and took a taxi for the last 50 miles.

At FOIC's office I found my appointment was to an almost new Hunt Class destroyer, HMS BROCKLESBY, which had been commissioned only six weeks before. The Hunts, named after the fox-hunting packs around the country, were a modern design around 1200 tons with a maximum speed of 27 knots and now coming into service. Eighty-six in total were built, the first being laid down in 1939 and the last in 1941. We carried four 4" HA/LA guns in director-controlled twin mountings instead of the designed six 4" guns for the Type 1, which for BROCKLESBY was found to be unstable with three mountings, so Bofors' pom-poms and Oerlikons filled the space. She was well fitted with depth charge throwers, radar and Asdic. The major design feature of having the officers' quarters and wardroom amidships instead

---

[14] Flag Officer in Charge

of aft as in older destroyers was a very practical innovation, enabling the officers to 'live on the job' instead of clawing their way along the 'iron deck' in heavy seas when going on watch. Similarly the gun crews lived adjacent to their gun mountings. Another odd feature was the fitting of stabilisers supposedly to provide a more stable gun platform. They were quite useless in service and in my experience never used except when entering harbour after a successful action when they could be switched on to make the ship roll and replicate the 'victory roll' of returning fighter aircraft! I think Messrs Denny Brown who designed and made these stabilisers must have had a good salesman close to the Royal Corps of Naval Constructors. I considered myself fortunate as the dreaded alternative going the rounds was an appointment to one of the 50 old ex-American 'four-stackers' now arriving from the US in exchange for a lease of bases in Bermuda and elsewhere in the Caribbean! They were notoriously uncomfortable.

After the usual hanging around in Milford Haven for a day or two BROCKLESBY arrived and I joined with my gear; a lean amount compared to the luggage I took east to DORSETSHIRE. Whilst I was still standing on the 'iron deck' waiting for someone to show me where I was to go, we moved off to a buoy and promptly went aground on the way. This I thought a bit strange but maybe it's what destroyers did. With no shouting but stirring up lots of mud we pulled clear and secured to a buoy.

The next day, 31st May, we slipped at 1000 and I had the first of many convoy escorting trips around Lands End to Falmouth and then on to Plymouth where I had a shock to see the sorry state it was in following the heavy bombing since I was last there a year before. Believe it or not we were going in for a boiler clean so I had again a few days leave, so I jumped on the 8.20 am at Plymouth and the long and weary journey to Glasgow which I reached 24 hours later. I ran into John Westmacott and Bernard Acworth outside the Central Hotel and over a few drinks heard a first hand account of the sinking of the BISMARCK on 27th May and the coup-de-grace by DORSETSHIRE.

Meeting up with Kirsteen at Aunt Bill's[15] I was perfectly on time

---

[15] Kirsteen's maiden aunt, Wilhelmina Brown.

for the move into Arnwood Drive where we slept for the first time that night, but then I was off a couple of days later for the long journey back south to Plymouth via Bristol getting aboard at 3.30am.

Apparently my call to BROCKLESBY was temporarily to replace a useless sub-lieutenant but the Captain, Lt Cdr George Huddart, asked if I would like to remain permanently - as I could envisage many worse billets I said *"yes"*. He phoned McDougall at the Admiralty and arranged it.

We sailed and arrived at Milford Haven at 1500 on 10th June and were bombed in harbour on the 11th having to spend all night on the bridge lashing out with the pom-poms. In the morning we set off with a convoy for Falmouth again being attacked from 0200 until daylight. Being trigger happy we shot up a Blenheim, which is similar to a JU88, coming in low on an attack bearing just after dawn but fortunately missed.

This was the pattern of our escort routine but it wasn't dull with BROCKLESBY proving to have a splendid crew of officers and men. George Huddart was a fun Captain always on for a party and the First Lieutenant, Loftus Peyton-Jones (P-J), has since then been a life-long friend of mine. His naval training and experience had ensured BROCKLESBY set off to a good start with excellent Standing Orders, Watch Bill, etc, in place which was of enormous help to me when eventually I took over from him as No 1. The Chief Petty Officer and Coxswain (the senior rating on board) whose action station was always the wheel in the wheelhouse was CPO McNaughton, a tough Scotsman whom I - almost alone amongst the crew - could understand.

On 20th June we put into Dartmouth; always the most enjoyable and attractive harbour on our 'beat', and after oiling I went ashore to join up with Kirsteen and Kenneth who had made the long and uncomfortable journey south on the chance of getting a few days together. Fortunately Kenneth was able to find out where BROCKLESBY would be ahead of time. We stayed ashore at the Royal Castle Hotel and, although I had to spend some time on board, we managed dinghy picnics up the Dart to Dittisham and after dinner on board we went up to the Naval College for a flick[16].

---

[16] film

Britannia Royal Naval College, the training ground for regular naval officers, had by now been evacuated to Eaton Hall in Cheshire but a skeleton staff remained and they made us very welcome to use the facilities.

Kirsteen was now well on with her pregnancy of 'Wee Johnnie' as we called 'it', which of course was the embryonic Sue due in November. She had made friends ashore with the wives of the other ships of our regular escort group so she had companionship while we were at sea. However she and Kenneth who was on leave went off back North on the 23rd. On our way to Milford Haven we spotted a smoking Blenheim diving into the sea about 8 miles off Plymouth however when we reached the spot there were no survivors.

As the Germans had by now occupied all the north and west of France there were Luftwaffe airfields established along the coast from where of course they harried our convoys. When at sea on convoy duty or even on passage in these waters we were at 'Defence Stations' which meant watch on – watch off every four hours and a maximum of $3^1/_2$ hours sleep at any one time. Added to this we went to 'Action Stations' at dawn and dusk as this was the time when the Luftwaffe made their sneaky attacks. Altogether it was a very tiring routine. The ME 109's and JU88 bombers could cross the Channel undetected beneath our radar beams ashore and on the escorts, and pounce with only a few minutes warning. As a result it became desirable to maintain a standing fighter patrol of a Spitfire or Hurricane circling round the convoy during daylight hours. Gradually we came to know the pilots and this developed into an exchange of visits. They came off for dinner and sometimes came out for a day at sea. Conversely we visited their airfields at Angle, Roborough and Milford Haven and had some cheery unconstrained nights. Characters I remember were a Prince Dimitri, a wild Polish pilot (they all were) and a Flt Lt Buchan, son of John Buchan the writer who was by then Governor-General of Canada and coincidentally a relation of P-J's.

On one such occasion I asked Sqn-Ldr Russell of 66 Squadron if he could spare a plane and pilot to fly me up to Glasgow should I have a weekend's leave. No problem to concur after a convivial evening.

He was as good as his word, so when we had boiler cleaning leave alongside in Plymouth on 24th July I phoned Russell and he organised me up to Roborough airfield where after a long delay and several drinks I took off at 1900 in a Lysander flown by a P/O Martin from Old Sarum to head for Abbotsinch and was fuzzily instructed on how to operate the parachute and the machine gun as *"there was a lot of enemy activity"*. When donning the parachute I inadvertently pulled the release clip and the whole parachute spilled out; we had not time to get a replacement so I bundled the lot into the cockpit with me and prayed it would open effectively if I had to jump out. At least it kept me warm. We refuelled at Preston before going on to Abbotsinch Airport arriving very late but still in the northern daylight at 2250. As we circled the airport ambulances came rolling out to greet us, as apparently the control tower wasn't expecting us and the barrage balloons had been sent up, rendering the airport theoretically impregnable and plane-proof. We landed safely but it was a bit alarming to see the balloon wires flashing past as we circled down in the Lysander. Thankfully Martin was quite unaware of the situation until we landed or he might have panicked. Kirsteen came down to meet us and Martin spent the night at Arnwood Drive. The next day I took him to Abbotsinch and he flew back to Old Sarum.

Mother was very ill after a recent operation for cancer and was in a nursing home but after seeing her over the next few days I had to get back to the ship. Kirsteen and I took the sleeper south on 29th July to Dartmouth where she again set up camp in the Royal Castle Hotel and I went on to the ship at Plymouth. We were now into August 1941 and it was fun having Kirsteen temporarily based in Dartmouth where she had the company of wives from the other ships of our escort flotilla.

This 15th DF based on Plymouth was a mixed bag of other Hunts such as CLEVELAND, TYNEDALE, FERNIE and the Polish manned KRACOVIAK, SLAZAK and KUJIWIAK as well as some old V & W destroyers; VETERAN with old friend Alistair Dow on board, VIVIEN with Tom Harvey and Tom Walkinshaw; and a clutch of armed anti-submarine trawlers including LADY ROSEMARY and DERBY COUNTY who were not much good at repelling the enemy but extremely useful as rescue vessels.

At this juncture in the war we were not troubled by U-boats or E-boats in our area but by ME 109s and JU88s coming in from France under the radar at any daylight hour, most frequently at dawn. Occasionally an Arado torpedo-carrying float-plane would position itself on a clear night in the lee of Lundy, or some such sheltered headland and attack the passing convoy. I don't record them having any success but they certainly frightened us. They were powered by 176hp BMW engines.

As with all destroyers there were plenty of varied diversions to keep us on our toes apart from Captain (D)[17] making sure we were busy at sea exercising the armament and the latest anti-submarine tactics being fed in from the eye of the storm at Western Approach Command at Liverpool.

One such successful sortie was on 9th July when following a night air raid on Dartmouth by ME 109s (which appeared to be directed particularly at ourselves with FERNIE alongside or so it seemed!) we were dispatched at 1430 to pick up a crashed Hudson crew off Ushant. At our maximum speed of 26 knots we met up with TYNEDALE off Land's End and an aircover escort of Hudsons until dusk. We went to action stations at 2300 in bright moonlight. At 0030 flares were seen from a Sunderland flying boat gently rocking on the sea; we went close to her at 0115 and, with our whaler in the charge of P-J, took off the crew of eleven Australians and four of the crashed Hudson's crew whom the Sunderland of No 10 Squadron from Pembroke had picked up earlier on their rescue mission. This situation was a chapter of accidents. The Hudson, on a surveillance sortie to Brest, had been shot down on her return flight but the crew were able to take to their rubber dinghy which had a radio beacon. The Sunderland was sent out to rescue them and located the dinghy on quite a calm sea but while landing to pick up the crew was severely damaged and couldn't take off. We then joined in the chain of events which included destroying the Sunderland with a 4" shell resulting in a spectacular display of exploding Verey lights and

---

[17] Captain (Destroyers): Captain of the Destroyer Flotilla e.g. Captain 17th DF

petrol in the clear moonlight night. Before destroying the Sunderland we relieved her of three Vickers machine guns which were a useful addition to our armament. We had been alerted to the possibility of a U-boat in the vicinity so together with FERNIE we carried out an Asdic box search in the area but to no avail. The aircrews were landed back at Plymouth after which we returned to Dartmouth to pick up a convoy at 5am on 11th July for a quiet trip to Falmouth. Routine leave was in the offing which meant quite a lot of work for me as one of my jobs was running the office involving the issuing of railway warrants, pay and organising a skeleton watch bill for the unfortunates required to remain on board. However a signal came in the evening to slip immediately so at midnight we set off to search for a U-boat reported laying mines off Land's End. This was abortive but we tacked ourselves onto a convoy heading for Milford Haven to provide extra security.

It was not until 24th July that we finally went on leave and I availed myself of the potentially suicidal flight to Abbotsinch recounted earlier. At the end of that leave Kirsteen joined me for a couple of days in London and then on to the Dartmouth where I was able to spend time with her between convoy trips. We managed a day and a night at the Imperial Hotel in Torquay which was redolent of peacetime with a band for dancing and seemingly plenty of food and drink available.

As best I could, in view of the difficulties with trunk calls, I kept in touch with home and the advance of my mother's final illness. In Falmouth on 12th August I managed to get through at 10.45pm, when I heard from Kenneth that mother had died that evening. George Huddart immediately granted me leave so I caught the 0955 train and met up with Kirsteen at Exeter and eventually on to Glasgow. Dad was bearing up well and there was a lovely funeral service for that fine woman who was the lynch pin and exemplar of a family of three rather wild, spoiled sons and a husband of Edwardian, if not of Victorian outlook and uncertain temper, at our family church, St Gilberts in Pollokshields. I was back on board in Dartmouth by the 17th. Fortunately there were no raids or panic sorties to sea and I was able to relax on board and contemplate on the first sad breach in our close family.

The routine convoys between the Solent and Milford Haven continued on a quiet note for some weeks: at the Solent-end we parted from our charges which were a mixed bag of coastal freighters including family manned Dutch schutjes, and almost always a couple of oil-tankers destined for the power stations at Southampton and Portsmouth - they were the jewels in the crown to be closely protected. While waiting for the return journey we anchored off Yarmouth on the Isle of Wight which was always a popular terminus offering pleasant pubs and walks ashore. Loftus Peyton-Jones, our 'Jimmy'[18], had an aunt who lived just outside Yarmouth where we enjoyed several tea-time visits; he also had cousins at Torquay where we were always made welcome for a brief taste of civilian life.

The 20th August 1941 passed, marking two years at war and my diary entry noted *"Faintly weary of it all but good for a long while yet!"* Little did I know it was two up and four to go! We were due for a boiler clean leave in early September but before that had another air sea rescue diversion to sweep for four air crew downed in the drink, but sadly had no luck in rescuing them. I was on duty for this spell of leave where we conveniently lay alongside Flagstaff Steps and the Captain also remained on board: we made the most of this time in Devonport and had several well contested games of golf at Yelverton followed on most evenings with a party of the local 'Boat Wrens' on board.

These 'Boat Wrens' are a little story of their own: Mrs Welby, Superintendent WRNS Plymouth Command, held the view that girls could replace sailors as crew on harbour craft and so release men for seagoing duties. She asked the Admiralty if she might try out a few selected Wrens and when this was agreed interviewing and training started. It was fairly demanding work for the girls as Devonport is a huge, quite exposed area of water, but soon it became commonplace to have the picket-boats that attended us in harbour manned by 'Boat Wrens' coming smartly alongside handling the boathooks, fenders and warps in a professional manner. They were dressed in bell-bottoms

---

[18] First Lieutenant and second-in-command of the ship

and jumpers when on duty and wore white lanyards as unofficial category badges. As you can imagine they came in for a tremendous amount of what is now called 'harassment' when they went to and fro around the ships in harbour but I never heard any of them complaining about the catcalls which they rightly accepted as a form of greeting. This elite group certainly didn't need any modern day 'counselling'!

BROCKLESBY, being based on Plymouth and a regular visitor there, soon developed excellent relations with some of these crews and our mail was alongside as soon as we were secured. We had many parties led by our extrovert Capt George Huddart with these 'Boat Wrens' on board and at the Saturday evening dances at the Moorland Links Hotel at Yelverton about 8 miles from Plymouth.

One of the Wrens, Cynthia Ratcliffe, was engaged to a RNVR doctor Alan McKelvie from Glasgow whom I knew well so I used to take her to these dances on the pillion of a motorbike I had bought for £5 and kept in the Dockyard. The girls all had at least one evening dress for these occasions and I recall well, not being allowed to forget it to this day, when on our way to the party at Moorland Links her one and only green dress - she was a redhead - was caught in the chain of the bike and was nearly ripped off her back. She eventually married McKelvie and they went to America after the war where he became a prominent surgeon in Washington DC. Years later they divorced and Cynthia is now married to Richard Helms, lately head of the CIA. Her portrait together with her shipmate Pauline Davidson on the boat they manned is hanging in the Imperial War Museum.

On 15th September we were making a fast passage from Milford Haven to Falmouth. I was well asleep after I had turned over the first watch to David Caley, when there was an almighty crash and howling of sirens: we had collided with the Dutch destroyer ISAAC SWEERS, both doing about 25 knots. Neither of us of course were showing navigation lights as we were blacked out. A large hole in the starboard side and damage to gun mountings resulted in poor David, a regular RN, having a rough time at the subsequent Court of Enquiry. We always received a routine signal of ships movements before sailing and the

ISAAC SWEERS should certainly have known of our convoy. After repairs in Falmouth we escorted two laden tankers to Portland amidst a steady stream of 'blue' air raid warnings which fortunately weren't aimed at us: then back to Devonport when it was time for a bit of leave coupled with an Asdic course at HMS OSPREY at Dunoon and HMS NIMROD at Campbeltown.

On the journey north on the 17th/18th September I met Hunter Roxburgh, Willis' brother, in Euston Station with his second wavy stripe up, on his way to join a Hunt class destroyer in the Mediterranean in which he was tragically killed by friendly fire at Christmas 1942. After the war his widow Joan married Willis.

After the usual exhausting journey standing up or sitting in the corridor of the trains I had a happy two days at home with Kirsteen, now very pregnant. I was then off on the course in the little Ford 8 we were running which was economical on the few gallons of petrol we were allowed. I met up with the McKersie family who lived in Campbeltown and who were running mates in our pre-war social pack. They owned a distillery there, had a lovely house called Auchinlea, and the girls were doing their bit at the Naval Base.

We conducted our Asdic training from the luxury yacht SHEMARA trying to detect an 'H' Class submarine, H-23, in the deep Kilbrannan Sound twixt Kintyre and Arran. H-23 was commanded by Lt Paul Skelton and I spent a day at sea in her, having the best lunch of the week and surprisingly suffered no sensation of claustrophobia. However I certainly wasn't attracted to service in submarines. I nipped back home at the weekend and resumed the course on the Monday. Finally after saying farewell to the McKersies, and with a welcome parting gift of grapes for Kirsteen from their Auchinlea greenhouses, I returned home late at night on the Friday.

Kenneth was home with our father at Erskine Avenue for the weekend from his sloop, HMS HUNTLEY, in Londonderry having just returned from an horrendous Atlantic convoy battle which lost eight ships out of twelve on the way home. He was having a rough time. He was applying to take the long 'G'[19] course at Whale Island and qualify as a Gunnery Officer - which eventually he did. On my part I intended to continue in the Navy as a 'Salt Horse'[20].

I had to leave at 10 o'clock the next day, 12th October, for London where I had dinner with my old friends the Easdales and then caught the sleeper from Paddington to Plymouth. Betty Easdale, an old girlfriend, had become engaged to an Indian Army officer. As BROCKLESBY wasn't in harbour I checked into the Barracks and on inquiring at Captain (D)'s office when she was expected, was told I wasn't required until the 22nd so I quickly turned around, caught the 1130am to London and arrived back in Glasgow at 7pm the next day! The prospect of having to spend six days in Devonport Barracks was most disagreeable. Making my way back to the ship I called in at Rex House at the Admiralty where I learnt I was to take over as No1 of BROCKLESBY with Loftus P-J shortly to be promoted to No1 of a Fleet destroyer. George Huddart had married on leave Stan Leslie, a Wren Cypher Officer from 'D' Watch of Western Approach Command, and was in great form as ever.

The routine convoy passages were resumed with the weather gradually moving into the autumnal gales making the shepherding of the ships, some of them small and slow, extremely difficult. These vessels dictated the speed and advance of the convoy round the Lizard, Land's End, Trevose Head and across the heavy tides of the Bristol Channel making it a difficult and exhausting task. The standing patrols by our guardian angels from the RAF kept the Luftwaffe off our backs but occasionally at night we were bothered by the Arado torpedo float planes lurking in the lee of Lundy Island.

With the pending departure of Loftus P-J our officer complement was augmented by the appointment of Mort Duffus, a tall Canadian RCNVR from Vancouver, who was a splendid addition to the mess

---

[19] Gunnery
[20] Non-specialist General Service Officer.

insofar as his arrival was followed by a regular supply of 'goodies' from Canada, and the amazing advent of his wife Johnnie, a Canadian Wren, to a posting in Devonport. They obviously had influence! He was so tall he had difficulty squeezing himself into the Director Control tower which was his action station. The morning after a party in the wardroom he often had a sticking plaster on his slightly bald head where the rough deckhead had come down and scraped him. He took over my job as foc'sle officer and understudied me in charge of the office, as I shadowed P-J to learn the No1's duties.

On a very wild night in November we had put into Portland and an old friend from DORSETSHIRE, Lt Herbert Acworth, known as 'A' and now happily in charge of the Hunt Class destroyer PUCKERIDGE came over for dinner and we talked 'old ships'. Back in Plymouth after a convoy the Captain's wedding present from the wardroom arrived which was presented after dinner filled with Drambuie and duly emptied. As a Lieutenant-Commander it was customary for the Captain to dine in the wardroom. A Captain of more exalted rank usually dined alone!

On 16th November we hit a gale force wind with snow and low visibility when rounding Land's End on the way to Milford Haven and, when in charge of the first watch, I lost touch with the convoy. Seas were the height of the bridge and no-one was allowed on the upper deck where lifelines were rigged as seas swept over it. When watches had to be changed the ship was turned pitching head into the seas and *"watches change"* was announced over the SRE. Eventually we made the lee of Lundy Island where we spent the day keeping anchor watches. The weather moderated on the 18th and we went on to Milford where we were relieved to find that the ships of the convoy had all found shelter although some were in other ports in the Bristol Channel.

A few days later, having returned to the Solent to oil and pick up another convoy for Falmouth, the same happened again and another gale caused the convoys' Commodore to heave-to the ships, leaving us to escort one tanker into Falmouth. As we entered Falmouth Roads a Heinkel III flew over making for the tanker but missed. We returned to Dartmouth at high speed as the Captain's bride was staying in the Royal

Castle Hotel. All this time our own 'Wee Johnnie' was overdue and at every opportunity I was leaping ashore to battle with the overloaded telephone system to Glasgow to obtain the latest bulletin on progress.

We departed again on 26th November to Milford Haven with a convoy and again hit dreadful weather. This didn't give us a chance to dry out the mess decks and restore some comfort below. When we arrived there it was still blowing so hard we had to put two bridles on the buoy and had no liberty boats in the water until the weather moderated. On the 28th we sailed at 1030 for Yarmouth and that night at 2200 were attacked by a Dornier flying boat which we drove off with the Bofors and Oerlikons, firing some 200 rounds,.

We reached Yarmouth, Isle of Wight at noon and after visiting P-J's aunt for tea, that included a fresh egg, I remained ashore in the Pier Hotel trying to put through a call home. This I eventually succeeded in doing to hear the great news of the birth of a daughter four days previously. As it was dark and the tides off Yarmouth were strong no liberty boats were running so I spent the night in the hotel. We were due for a boiler cleaning leave, but this was delayed by having to escort some tankers from Milford Haven to Plymouth so it was 8.00 pm on 6th December before I reached home to see Kirsteen and Susanne for the first time. We had a very happy few days together with both families celebrating, during which Willis, now in 206 Squadron Coastal Command, came up from Prestwick where he had been forced down by bad weather on his way to his base in Belfast. I also managed to contact Kenneth in Belfast where he had just returned from Freetown on a convoy escort job - on this occasion they had only lost one ship.

Glasgow Herald, 28th November 1943
Daughter Sue's Birth Announcement

MILLER.- At Landrick, 9 Arnwood Drive, Glasgow, W.2. on 27th November, 1941, to Kirsteen (née Orr), wife of Lieutenant Alan J. M. Miller, R.N.V.R., a daughter; both well.

I was back on board by 12th December but the weather was so bad that the merchant ships were not prepared to leave harbour and this was compounded by having a dynamo break down: it was most unusual to have a defect like this. However I was able to book some satisfactory calls home to check that all was well and cast around for Christmas presents in Plymouth but the shops were nearly empty of coupon free merchandise. We eventually sailed on the 18th in good weather for a change, oiled at the Shell-Mex jetty in the Hamble and picked up a convoy for Milford, en route having to beat off a persistent attack by a couple of Heinkel 115 float-planes.

David Caley, our delightful Sub Lt, shipped his second stripe and was off to the Clyde to stand by a destroyer building at Yarrows: his replacement, Dansie, another RN Sub Lt joined the previous day. As we had lots of room at Arnwood Drive and a couple of Highland lassies as maids, Kirsteen offered to put David up for a few weeks until his ship was ready. This worked out well and he was a great support and companion for her especially when the maids walked out! In uniform he used to push Susanne out in her pram at weekends; good grist for the neighbours' gossip mill!

After a quiet trip to Milford, we were back anchored off Yarmouth on Christmas Day and after a traditional tour of the mess decks and rum with the Petty Officers, I had a sharp walk to Freshwater with P-J and a Christmas Dinner on board in the evening, turning in at 2am. New Years Day was spent in Plymouth, with the Captain organising a Wrens party on board and sixteen bells struck at midnight. Some masochistic staff officer had ordered a practice shoot for us at sea the next day and we were all delighted when neither aircraft nor target appeared allowing us to creep thankfully back into the Sound to anchor and sleep.

Chapter VII

BROCKLESBY'S NO 1 - ENGLISH CHANNEL
January 1942

I t was now January 1942 and indications of changes to our close knit and well run ship were evident; the principal one being a ciphered signal appointing George Huddart captain of a Fleet destroyer HMS FORESTER, operating on the 'Russian Run' escorting convoys from Scapa Flow to Murmansk. He was destined to be killed in her a few months later in May in the Barents Sea defending convoy QP11 and HMS EDINBURGH against German destroyers and U-boats. An archetypal destroyer captain if ever there was one: professional, charismatic and trustworthy. His pending departure from BROCKLESBY left a sense of uneasiness. Who would we get next?

On the list of tasks was an imminent refit which would mean the drafting of experienced ratings and petty officers to other ships to leaven the complements of the many new ships coming into service.

So to Portsmouth to de-ammunition and then into the Ocean Dock at Southampton to start the refit by Harland and Wolff. A ship in dock is at best very uncomfortable but this occasion was compounded by snow, cold weather and air raids, so following the conference with FOIC's staff and Harland and Wolff's yard management, it was a relief to go off on leave. My diary has 'on leave' blank pages until 23rd January when I left home with Kirsteen for Southampton where we set up camp in the gloomy Royal Hotel.

A few days later our new Captain, Lt Michael Tufnell DSC, a battle hardened RN Lieutenant with six years seniority joined us; he had been No1 of the Hunt Class destroyer HMS ATHERSTONE operating in the hostile waters of the Nore Command in the North Sea and Dover Straits so he had plenty of active experience to bring to us.

The refit dragged on but we did achieve some useful improvements such as an updated 293 radar accompanied by three trained 'Headache' operators, of which more later, who added to the already crowded messdeck; a winch appeared on the quarter-deck to handle the new idea of escorts sporting a barrage balloon to discourage enemy aircraft. These would be handed out to the escorts like balloons at a children's party as we left harbour and when they were hoisted to 1000 feet the effect was quite festive. They had a mind of their own if a head wind of 20 knots was added to the ships speed!

After a little liquid negotiation with the Yard manager I had all the officers bunks replaced with mattresses from the first class cabins of the QUEEN MARY which, now being a troopship, had multibunk cabins and these luxuries were in store ashore.

The ship's officers were sent off on gunnery and ASDIC courses. After Susanne's christening ceremony in Westbourne Church, Glasgow on 8th February and attendant celebrations I went south again for a Gunnery course at Whale Island. It was while there that the successful breakout of the SCHARNHORST, GNEISENAU and PRINCE EUGEN from Brest up through the Channel and Straits of Dover to the safety of the Elbe, took place. Our late detection and hastily improvised counter-measures with MTBs and Swordfish torpedo aircraft of the destroyer- and Messerschmitt-escorted German squadron was a disastrous failure and a humiliating naval experience. All six Swordfish were shot down, and the MTBs from Dover under the command of Lt Cdr Nigel Pumphrey DSO DSC (later to be our Captain) never had a hope of getting close to the battleships through the screen of destroyers and E-boats, although they most gallantly attacked. The only damage to the enemy ships was by our mines when approaching the Elbe.

It was 20th February before we were clear of the dockyard and had a work-up in the Solent to exercise our armament and try out the new equipment before resuming our convoy escort duties in the western English Channel. It took four days to sort out the dockyard mess and have BROCKLESBY ship-shape again. By now our flotilla had adopted the variegated pastel camouflage painting of the hull and upperworks purported to be a recommendation of the wildlife painter, Peter Scott; it was designed to break up the hard silhouette of a vessel and was quite

Clyde Division RNVR Officers en route to the Far East aboard HMT *Dunera* in August 1939 - left to right: Charlie Dobson, Alick Kennedy, James Matheson, and Bob Pattman

The *Walrus* seaplane ready for launch aboard HMS Dorsetshire

Recovery from the St Nazaire Raid 28th March 1942 - HMS Brocklesby with ML - 314 alongside.

HMS *Dorsetshire*, County Class cruiser and the author's first ship, in the South Atlantic in 1940

attractive into the bargain[21]. These camouflage painting designs were widely adopted throughout the fleet. Peter Scott was also making a name for himself in the steam gunboats (SGBs) of Coastal Forces. They were based at Dartmouth and on several occasions lay alongside us, where he and his officers had the courtesy of our wardroom. We found him a rather morose and serious character and, in fact, a bit of a bore. The SGBs built by William Denny of Dumbarton, were proving a bit temperamental to achieve operational reliability and their high-pressure superheated Yarrow boilers were lethal when they were hit.

Loftus Peyton-Jone's appointment as No1 of the Fleet destroyer ACHATES, based on Scapa Flow and deployed escorting convoys to Russia, came through and he left us at Falmouth on 2nd March after a splendid farewell party that lasted until early in the morning. So now I was First Lieutenant and second-in-command - quite a responsibility particularly as our new Captain, Mike Tufnell, hadn't yet had an opportunity to 'show his mettle' to the officers and men of his command.

It wasn't long before that time came. After a convoy trip to Milford Haven and back to Cowes, plagued by plenty of enemy aircraft passing overhead and generating tiring 'Red' alerts a signal came to proceed to Dartmouth at best speed. Arriving at 1800 on 5th March, we were off at 1850 for Alderney with two MLs in company taking up a patrol line 2 miles off the French coast which we held until 0300 - all very tense as an enemy convoy was reported to have two destroyers for protection. There was no contact or sign of the enemy so we had to break off at 0320 and head back to the English coast before daylight brought out the Luftwaffe on top of us. I was on the bridge all night until 0600 when we picked up our east-going convoy off Portland and took it through to Cowes. Later that same day we sailed for Falmouth with a west bound convoy! This hectic schedule was the pattern for March and as No1 I even took my first Church of England service one Sunday on the for'd messdeck and Divisions on the following Sunday. Other odd but interesting duties seemed to come with the job; such as sitting

---

[21] In fact these designs and colours were used in the First World War.

on a Selection Board with Captain (D) for Commissioned Warrant (CW) candidates[22].

The weather was uniformly bad almost all month with gales and fog. This added to the pressure of shepherding the convoys: on the 20th March we left Dartmouth to pick up a Milford convoy in thick fog in Mounts Bay; when this difficult manoeuvre was completed and we were passing Trevose Head at dusk there was a very determined attack by a Dornier 215 and a couple of JU 67s (dive bombers). A mass of lead went up from the escorts bringing down the Dornier and one JU67. After four attacks they had sunk the freighter, R105Y, but all the crew were saved; there were no survivors from the downed enemy aircraft.

At the end of one eastward convoy we berthed in Portsmouth, now sorely battered, and I sent a signal to Kenneth doing his long 'G' course at 'Whaley' (the Naval Gunnery School on Whale Island at the head of Portsmouth Harbour) and he came aboard for a few hours one evening arriving in his latest 1 $\frac{1}{2}$ litre MG Roadster - a proper MG, not a 'badged' Morris. This gave me an opportunity to hear of his harrowing experiences in 1941 when in the ancient coal-burning sloop, HMS PANGBOURNE, running the convoys from Alexandria to the beleaguered garrison of Tobruk which could only be supplied and maintained by sea. With the Germans having airfields and aircraft within a few miles of Tobruk and coastal batteries along the coast commanding the entrance to the harbour, the ships could only arrive under cover of darkness, discharge during the night and sail again before daylight. The casualty list of ships and men on this desperate lifeline to maintain the garrison and supply forward military units grew more difficult as time went on. Eventually Tobruk had to be evacuated between 17th-21st June 1941 although many of the troops and small ships in harbour had to be abandoned. It was not until November 1942 during the rapid advance westwards of the Eighth Army that Tobruk was recaptured.

---

[22] Other ranks who were identified with potential for commissioning became CW candidates and wore a white band on their caps.

Chapter VIII

THE ST NAZAIRE RAID
27 – 29 March 1942

On the evening of 25th March we slipped Cowes to await our westbound convoy and Mike Tufnell went ashore to the usual convoy Commodore's conference while a few of us visited the Fountain Hotel for a pint or two; little did I know how familiar this hostelry would become in the years ahead.

While at sea a signal came to put into Falmouth where we collected sealed orders and, in company with HMS CLEVELAND under the command of Cdr Sayer as Senior Officer, set off in support of the assault force of HMS CAMBELTOWN, MLs and MTBs, in a daring and carefully planned attack by Commandos on the Normandie Dock complex at St Nazaire situated at the mouth of the Loire in the Bay of Biscay. CinC Plymouth had also received information that five enemy torpedo boats of the Mowe Class had been reported off St Nazaire *"and might be met"*. The assault force had a couple of Hunts, ATHERSTONE and TYNEDALE, already with them but these would not have sufficient clout to deal with the enemy destroyers should they be encountered.

The raid was brilliantly successful, although the casualties amongst the Commandos and naval crews of the actual assault craft were heavy. I recommend anyone to read the detailed accounts of the action subsequently published but I will confine this narrative to our involvement in the raid.

The port of St Nazaire was one of the principal French shipbuilding centres, which in 1935 built the NORMANDIE then the largest passenger liner in the world, and incidentally one of the many large French and Italian passenger liners on which our family firm, Miller Insulation, laid the proprietary deck coverings. St Nazaire was of course now in enemy hands and the Normandie Dock was capable of dry-docking the German battleships such as the BISMARCK or

TIRPITZ. The objective of the raid was to destroy the docks to prevent their use by these ships. The Germans had also developed other areas of the docks as reinforced U-boat pens, although their destruction was a secondary target for the raid.

On the passage south HMS TYNEDALE with the Force Commander, Lt Cdr Ryder, on board spotted the conning tower of a U-boat which dived after being fired at, but was not depth charged as neither escorting destroyer could leave the raiding force. They wrongly assumed they had not been spotted but in fact, as I established after the war from a German biography, this returning U-boat reported *"three destroyers and ten MTBs making for the French coast"*. Early the next morning U-boat Command ordered *"all U-boats to the east of 29º W to make fastest speed to grid square BF6510 as the English had landed at St Nazaire"*.

The spearhead of the mission was a former American destroyer renamed HMS CAMBELTOWN, reinforced with armour plating against gunfire and loaded with explosives. In simple terms she was to be sailed up the Loire and driven into the lock gates of the Normandie Dock, there to explode.

To augment the protective escort we were instructed to rendezvous with TYNEDALE and ATHERSTONE on the morning of 28th March when the MLs and MTBs were turning for home after the attack, which in the event took place four minutes after the intended time when CAMBELTOWN hit the Dock and mounted the caisson.

The sea was calm and it was a moonlit night with low cloud as we rounded Ushant and at 0900 met up with TYNEDALE and ATHERSTONE who had had a brush with the five Mowe Class torpedo boats earlier at 0630. TYNEDALE was hit but the inconclusive action was broken off at 0645 when the enemy surprisingly made off to the south.

By this time of course the Luftwaffe was alerted and began to fill the air with Heinkel IIIs and Junker 88's. One of our Beaufighters which was providing air cover about 40 miles offshore collided before our eyes with a JU88 and both crashed into the sea with no survivors. Other enemy air attacks were kept up all day. BROCKLESBY shot down two JU88's with our 4" HA using the newly developed proximity fuses and discouraged several other air attacks on ourselves and the battered MLs we were shepherding for the homeward journey. Eventually we were ordered to persuade the crews of the MLs to abandon their boats, scuttle them and come home on board us.

Daily Telegraph, 31ˢᵗ March 1942

> H.M.S. Brocklesby has shot down one Junker 88 for certain with a direct hit from a 4in shell and has also probably destroyed another, the Admiralty announced yesterday.
>
> The second 'plane was hit many times by pom-poms, and then its nose was lifted by a four-inch shell which burst close under it.
>
> No casualties or damage were suffered by H.M.S. Brocklesby.

We were flying our battle ensign, about which more later, and remained at action stations all day while we searched for the battered MLs. After taking off the crews with many injured and dying, which our Doc Healey and the sick-bay attendants dealt with as best they could, we scuttled MLs 270, 446 and 314. It had been on ML 314, the Headquarters vessel, that Able Seaman Savage continued heroically to man the Bofors pom-pom in an endeavour to silence enemy fire from a pillbox on the old Mole until he was killed. He was awarded a posthumous VC for his gallant determination. When ML 314 was alongside us I went aboard to persuade the crew to come aboard BROCKLESBY. The scene below decks was truly a nightmare. The men were sitting around in cataleptic shock and didn't respond in any way to my request. Even when I ordered them they didn't move so I went back on board BROCKLESBY, drew a revolver, returned to ML 314 and, waving the gun, ordered them to bestir themselves and move aboard. This they did after which we scuttled her. Able Seaman Savage was not buried at sea in the traditional manner but was taken to Falmouth for burial ashore. Shipmates subscribed to buy his VC which is now in the national Maritime Museum at Greenwich.

By this time I and the other officers had been awake and active for over 36 hours; it was my first experience of taking Benzedrine to cope with these circumstances. To add to this Mike Tufnell was in a pretty bad way, never leaving the bridge and hardly allowing me to leave his side although it was my responsibility to move around the ship and ensure that all was in working order. Furthermore with the tension, which the flying of a battle ensign intensifies, I had to be seen to be around.

It was later learnt that a force of over a hundred bombers had been dispatched from Holland to intercept us and at 1400 when they were bombing up at Rennes aerodrome, our force of four destroyers, having done our mopping up, set off at increased speed for home so that, in the fortuitously low cloud cover, the bombers never made contact. To compound this bit of good fortune the large Blohm and Voss shadowing aircraft had been shot down by one of our Beaufighters and therefore could not re-direct this bomber force towards us.

Mention should be made of the contribution of the RAF. A diversionary raid by seventy bombers over the target was timed to coincide with the assault force's arrival at St Nazaire and whilst this was achieved, in effect it only served to raise the alarm and alert the defences as the sky was completely overcast and scarcely a bomb was dropped. By Cabinet decision targets in Occupied France were not to be bombed unless the weather permitted them to be identified clearly so in the event the air support by the RAF was a disadvantage. On the other hand during the withdrawal from St Nazaire the Luftwaffe failed, due to the cloud cover, to inflict any casualties on the rather scattered fleet returning from halfway down the Bay of Biscay. This was mainly due to the air cover provided by Beaufighters, Blenheims and Hudsons from our friends at St Eval who flew twenty-two sorties during which at least five enemy aircraft were shot down for the loss of two of ours. BROCKLESBY added two to this toll with Mort Duffus directing the guns from the most uncomfortable direction control tower (DCT) for hours at a time.

We reached Plymouth safely on the 29th and started our delayed short boiler cleaning which was extended as we had to dock for repairs to a defective stern gland. This ate into my leave and I didn't get away until Thursday 2nd April having to return on Saturday by the 9.30pm night sleeper. We were also having trouble with a gun-mounting which rendered us non-operational for some days more until it was fixed.

During this time Mike Tufnell came to see me to discuss the problem we had all observed and which I had been greatly concerned about during the St Nazaire operation, namely that he was suffering from what in these days we called 'anxiety neuroses' and nowadays 'post-traumatic stress'. He welcomed my suggestion to consult a Surg-Cdr who came on board. Following this Mike was ordered to relinquish his command of BROCKLESBY immediately and go on sick leave. In time he was fully recovered, not least by the tender care of his fine wife Patsy, and resumed his successful career in the Navy serving in aircraft carriers and promoted to Captain.

This posed a problem on BROCKLESBY as I wasn't qualified to assume command of a major war vessel so Peter Gretton was drafted in as our temporary captain having been given half-an-hour's notice by Captain (D) to collect his gear and get aboard BROCKLESBY as we were due to sail within the hour. Having commanded SABRE, his first command, an old and small First World War destroyer tasked with convoy duties in the Atlantic, he had then been appointed to WOLVERINE presently refitting in Devonport but she wasn't to be ready for a few weeks.

He came aboard as Mike Tufnell was still on his way ashore in a hospital pinnace and went straight up to the bridge when I reported *"Ready for sea"*. We slipped from the buoy and steamed out into Plymouth Sound in thick fog - a 'pierhead jump' if ever there was one. Peter wasn't a complete stranger as he had been aboard to our parties from time to time; in the beginning he appeared a bit of a misogynist and didn't quite approve of our 'Boat Wrens' who after all were 'ratings' and out of place larking around a wardroom. We soon softened him up and eventually he married a Wren.

On the other hand he was a tough and exacting Captain and I can truthfully say he was the most able naval officer I ever sailed with. He had every discipline required at his finger tips, being able for instance to read signals from an Aldis lamp concurrently with the Yeoman - something I never remotely accomplished.

He did a few routine uneventful convoy trips with us; the only diversion was to south of the Scilly Islands to escort a Union Castle Liner, the LLANGIBBY CASTLE which had her rudder blown off by a torpedo and was steering rather erratically by means of her propellers.

The few weeks Peter Gretton spent with us had a marked effect on BROCKLESBY; personally I realised the standards that could be achieved and learnt much from his short tenure and unbridled keenness. He of course went on in WOLVERINE and DUNCAN to be one of the great Escort Group Commanders of the vital U-boat war in the Atlantic and post-war to rise to be a Vice Admiral and Second Sea Lord.

Although we only served together for a few weeks we became good friends and after the war ended kept in touch until his too early death. I'm quite proud of the following extract from a letter he wrote to a mutual acquaintance in 1981 *"BROCKLESBY seemed to me to be a good ship and I thought the First Lieutenant was first class. But I record, if I am to be honest, that I found her not so much on her toes as she should have been"*. As I said his standards were exacting.

On Peter's last day with us when we were back in Plymouth I had the minor satisfaction of having a round of golf with him on a lovely day at Yelverton and beating him on the last green with a birdie three!

News came on 16th April that our new Captain was to be Lt Cdr Nigel Pumphrey DSO DSC who already had a distinguished career in MTBs. Amongst other exploits as I mentioned earlier he had led the MTBs and MGBs in the hopeless attack on the SCHARNHORST, GNEISENAU and PRINCE EUGEN as they passed up Channel in the breakout from Brest. He joined that evening to what was his first destroyer command.

Chapter IX

E-BOATS – 'SCHNELLBOOTE'
9 July 1942

Although E-boats had been operating against our East Coast convoys and in the Straits of Dover for many months in what was known as 'E-boat alley' they had not been stationed or active in the Western Channel. This was to change in the summer of 1942 when intelligence reported two flotillas were now based at Cherbourg.

These E-boats were, in almost every sense, superior to our MTBs and MGBs - they were about 115 feet long, carried torpedoes, had heavier armament (20mm Oerlikons and a 37mm gun), and were faster, being capable of 40 knots. But their principle advantage was their diesel powered engines (3000hp supercharged Daimler-Benz V-form diesels) less prone than our petrol driven boats (originally Italian Isotta Fraschini then Rolls Royce or Packard) to blow up or go on fire when hit. On the other hand our MTBs now had radar sets.

To combat this potential threat to our convoys we had, as previously mentioned, embarked three 'Special Operators' and fitted radio sets known as 'Headache' to intercept command orders being exchanged in German between the attacking E-boats. These Special Operators were university language graduates put into uniform and drafted aboard.

The convoy routine between Portsmouth and Milford Haven with stages to Dartmouth, Devonport and Falmouth continued with Nigel Pumphrey settling in well. Although BROCKLESBY was his first destroyer command he was an experienced seagoing naval officer having served in a variety of ships including DORSETSHIRE pre-war on the China Station. He was an interesting and expansive personality in the wardroom mess and fitted in well with our reputation for sociability.

The nature and character of a new commanding officer is of vital importance to all on board: our destiny is dependent on his judgement in action so in the beginning, especially if arriving with a good reputation, he is given whole hearted enthusiastic support which if he fulfils expectations makes for an efficient and 'happy' ship. The opposite is equally true; if a ships company has no confidence in the commanding officer, morale drifts low; 'toothsucking' and ill-discipline soon sour the atmosphere. Conversely the Captain has to have confidence in his officers and, as destroyers carried the minimum necessary to function effectively, everyone has to pull their weight. If he considered someone is not up to their job, a visit to Captain (D) quickly had him replaced.

As the days were getting longer enemy air activity increased so to counter and discourage this, our friendly air cover was augmented during the frequent alerts and we often had a couple of fighters patrolling up and down and around the convoy - it must have been a boring job for the pilots: maybe they thought the same about us. However the safe arrival of a convoy was our joint objective whatever the pressures.

There were other changes to the wardroom; a young Sub Lt Alistair Gilchrist joined us who had earned his commission as an Upper Yardsman[23], indicating he was pretty smart. He was a Scot whose father was the manager or owner of the Kingshouse Hotel at Glencoe which I knew well. A nice Irish Surg-Lt also joined us to replace the pleasant but lazy Doc Healey.

The regular boiler cleaning recess came around which gave us all a spell of leave so I shot up in the space of 30 hours to Glasgow for a few days. This coincided with David Caley's commissioning party of his new Hunt, HMS OAKLEY, of which he was No1. Loftus P-J, from ACHATES presently in Greenock, was also there. We had a great party with Kirsteen and others in Arnwood Drive finishing up in the familiar Piccadilly Club in Glasgow; better than battering our way round Land's End twice a week.

King George and Queen Elizabeth visited Plymouth on 7th May and our officers and others paraded on the depot ship PARIS where I

---

[23] Commissioned from the Lower Deck

was presented to the King. Meanwhile Queen Elizabeth was taken round Plymouth Harbour from Flagstaff Steps by a 'Boat Wren' crew in a highly polished barge.

Between convoys we spent much time exercising our armament off Plymouth with sub-calibre shoots, towed targets both floating and airborne, and anti-submarine tactics together with another Hunt stalking the submarine THUNDERBOLT as our quarry. Increasingly we carried out landing exercises with Commandos in landing craft - we had a feeling this presaged more St Nazaire type raids although at that time a full scale invasion wasn't thought of. Sometimes I was 'on the go' from 0400 to 1230 the next night - very wearing.

On 16th May in company with CLEVELAND we had just passed the Devonport gate in the boom at 1245 on our way to yet another exercise when, without any warning, four ME109Fs came whipping in at masthead height from astern firing their machine guns and cannon. We were not at action stations but our Yeoman of Signals who was at his usual post on the bridge, with the most amazing alertness and initiative jumped down to the lookout platform at the side of the bridge, cocked the Oerlikon and opened up on one of the 109's which crashed smoking into Cawsand Bay. We had a couple of seamen, Norridge and Aherne, quite badly injured by canon fire: the exercise for that day was called off. A cannon shell had gone through the legs of my No1 trousers hanging over the back of a chair in my cabin below the bridge which made for a good story at a party.

There was sad news of George Huddart's death in the Barents Sea whilst defending convoy QP11 returning from Murmansk with the cruiser HMS EDINBURGH which had earlier been torpedoed. He was killed on the bridge of his ship, HMS FORESTER, in the battle with three large German destroyers one of which, the HERMANN SCHOEMAKIN, was sunk. The First Lieutenant, Bitmead, took over command and after further encounters eventually brought FORESTER back to Scapa Flow. EDINBURGH finally sank and is now a War Grave lying at the bottom of the Barents Sea.

On one of our visits to Portsmouth I borrowed Kenneth's smart

M.G. when he was busy at Whaley and together with Mort Duffus paid a visit to Mike Tufnell who was now convalescing at their lovely home at Curdridge about 20 miles up the A30. He was well on the way to recovery.

It was noticeable when in Portsmouth towards the end of May that there was a growing concentration of new landing craft in the harbour which confirmed there was another raid afoot. However we carried on with our convoy escort routine and I note from my diary that for this time of year the weather was persistently bad - on one occasion we were the sole escort to Brixham of a single tanker which was urgently required there - our trawler and ML consorts could not accompany us due to the weather.

My DSC was gazetted on 22nd May and as we were going down Channel bound for Milford Haven with our convoy, PUCKERIDGE passed us, escorting the new Dido Class cruiser SIRIUS, and her Captain, Acworth, my old chum from DORSETSHIRE flashed across *'congrats on gong'.*

Glasgow Herald, Friday 29th May 1942

Glasgow Officer Wins D.S.C.

It is announced that Lieutenant Alan John McCulloch Miller, R.N.V.R, has been awarded the D.S.C. "for courage and skill in successful actions against enemy aircraft in H.M.S. Brocklesby."

Lieutenant Miller was in business in Glasgow as an engineer before the war along with his brother, Mr. Kenneth B. Miller, who is also now an officer in the R.N.V.R. He played Rugby for Kelvinside Academicals.

Lieutenant Miller has seen service abroad on a cruiser, and he took part in the St Nazaire exploit. His wife resides at Arnwood Drive, Kelvinside.

We received a rude awakening at dawn on 10th June when we were crossing Lyme Bay - two waves of JU87 dive bombers delivered a determined attack on the eight ships of the convoy and dropped some twenty bombs without doing any serious damage. The combined fire of the escorts shot down one plane and another headed back to France trailing smoke - certainly a 'probable'. There was no damage to any of our ships.

Kirsteen had been alerted about our impending leave and, having a good nanny at home to look after Sue, set off on the ghastly journey south to Plymouth where I met her off the 3.30 and made for the haven of the Moorland Links Hotel. It was a Saturday 13th June, when the hotel staged its ever popular weekly dance and life at that moment was quite delightful. She was wearing a white dress - probably her chopped off wedding dress! A few days earlier I had slipped and fallen on the 'iron deck' in the waist of the ship and struck my coccyx on the coaming of a hatch. This was extremely painful but I expected it to ease off and go away in a few days - however it didn't and the Doc sent me into Stonehouse Hospital for an examination; they wanted to keep me in. With Kirsteen around, this I had no intention of agreeing to, and we carried on making the most of our leave which included bussing to the Imperial Hotel in Torquay for a party with the Duffus's and a couple of Canadian RAF types and their floosies. Next day back on board an order came from Stonehouse that I had to go to Barrow Gurney Hospital for treatment - an agonising five hour bus journey on a hard seat. Barrow Gurney had its amusing features - it was a 'looney-bin' commandeered by the Navy for surgical cases. There were no locks on the loo doors or hooks on which you might hang yourself - very quaint. Again they wanted to keep me in for treatment but I told the Surg-Cdr (a specialist in a white coat) that I would come at a more convenient time and after one night there I walked out the door and hitch-hiked back to Plymouth - 136 miles in four hours. After reporting on board I went off immediately to the Moorland Links where Kirsteen was enjoying the lovely weather. However she had to return to Glasgow so after seeing her off on the 8.30am train, we sailed at 0900 for a couple of days of exercise shoots at sea. I was turning over to Mort Duffus as temporary No 1 in view of my pending hospitalisation at Barrow Gurney. This was to be soon but again I postponed it to enable Mort to go on leave with his wife Johnnie who had arrived from Canada, so I did another round convoy trip before going in to hospital. On 6th July we were in Milford Haven when it was mined by aircraft overnight delaying our departure with the return convoy while the port was swept. We did sail eventually in a summer gale and rain. Another flight of mine-laying planes came in at dusk of which one was downed by the shore ack-ack guns.

By Wednesday evening, the 9th, we were well on our way crossing Lyme Bay with the eastbound convoy of about ten ships - the usual mixture of tankers and coasters shepherded by ourselves and four armed trawlers. Shortly before darkness fell we spotted a shadowing aircraft to seaward and at 2300 a 'Blue' warning signal was received indicating a possible air attack. This did not materialise so we stood down from action stations and I turned in again, being due to take the morning watch at 0400 - the regular traditional watch for the First Lieutenant.

However at 0130 the alarm clanged and we went to action stations having been alerted by a stream of radio telephone traffic in German intercepted by our 'Headache' operators. This was the forerunner of the long anticipated E-boat onslaught on our PW/WP[24] convoys.

Nigel Pumphrey, our Captain, having previously been very active in Coastal Forces was familiar with E-boat tactics. As the enemy's orders to attack, translated from German, were relayed to him on the bridge we had a useful tactical advantage. However the onslaught by five E-boats proved to be beyond the limited fire-power and speed of one destroyer and four armed trawlers to rebuff.

The night fortunately was calm and from the plot of our PPI[25] radar and the star-shell barrage we laid bare the manoeuvres of the enemy. Their targets of course, as with the U-boats, were the merchant ships and only incidentally the escorts. They pressed their attack into

---

[24] Convoy routes: Portsmouth–West, West-Portsmouth.

[25] Plan Position Indicator.

the body of the convoy and let loose their torpedoes at the larger freighters, and at the same time ripping into them with their powerful 37mm and 20mm cannons. Multi-coloured tracer shells and our 4" star shells lit up the turmoil as we did our best to drive them off. However their torpedoes had found their marks and sank six ships including the precious oil-tanker PARMELLA which had sailed unmolested all the way from Curaçao. Fortunately the E-boat's torpedoes hit for and aft and didn't explode the cargo of benzine. She sank on an even keel. Ourselves, the other escorts, and merchant ships had anti-aircraft Oerlikons and machine guns which all joined in the defence, but despite many observed hits none of the E-boats was sunk or stopped. A direct hit by even one of our 4" shells would have knocked one out. Eventually we drove them off but with their superior speed they soon faded beyond the range of our star shell illumination to return to Cherbourg after which we, together with the trawler escorts, set about picking up the survivors. Altogether 85 seamen were rescued, some with serious injuries. Although BROCKLESBY was sprayed with cannon shell we had no casualties, the major damage being to the NAAFI canteen housed in the after deckhouse. Mars Bars and similar goodies were plastered over the bulkheads inside and the NAAFI manager was able at a stroke to reconcile any stock shortages in his returns.

Continuing with the reassembled remainder of our convoy I was wearily on watch at dawn when, without radar warning from shore or on board, four ME109Es came flashing low over the horizon and bombed another small ship to the bottom of the sea. We opened fire on the attackers but they all escaped although HMT CORNELIAN claimed to have shot one down. That was a cruel blow but there was another bitter ironic twist to the whole disastrous night when, as we approached the Needles at the west end of the Solent, the Coastguard Station flashed a message *"Where is your convoy?"*

This engagement was a major setback for us and I had a long meeting with Nigel Pumphrey to analyse our weaknesses and how best to ensure protection for the PW/WP convoys in the Western Channel now that the E-boats from Cherbourg were on the offensive and following this initial success would surely strike again. As previously mentioned we knew they were now stationed there and with the Navy's experience on the East coast convoy routes we should have been more aware of their threat and organised earlier counter-measures.

Nigel's own experience in Coastal Forces advocated the provision of nimble and fast MGBs to challenge the E-boats as they made their sortie from their new base in Cherbourg. It was impractical to have them as part of the convoy escort which bumbled along at 7 knots for days on end. Whether or not BROCKLESBY's proposals influenced the CinC to adopt these new tactics I don't know but they were put in place immediately with the transfer of the 8th MGB Flotilla from the Dover area now to be based at Dartmouth. This flotilla was commanded by Lt Cdr Robert Hitchens RNVR, the most famous figure in the history of Coastal Forces who in his brilliant but tragically short career had been decorated with the DSO and Bar and the DSC and two Bars.

The MGBs of Hitchen's 8th Flotilla were the latest more heavily armed 'seventy-two-foot-six' boats and the night following arrival at Dartmouth, which of course was one of our staging posts on the convoy route, Hitchens had gone on the offensive. Our confrontation with the E-boats had been on 9th July. By the night of 14th July he was lying in wait with three MGBs 12 miles north of Alderney for the E-boats to emerge from Cherbourg or St Peter Port. They didn't come out that night but instead the MGBs encountered a tanker escorted by two large armed trawlers which were immediately attacked, with Hitchins cutting across the bows of the tanker and dropping a depth charge as he passed - a manoeuvre he had previously used to effect. This set the tanker on fire but his boat was badly damaged by gunfire from the tanker and escorts and two of his crew were killed.

However on 1st August when repeating this tactic of lying in wait off the E boats lair like a terrier at a burrow, the MGBs received a signal that the E-boats had earlier left Cherbourg and were making for our coast. The night became foggy. Although Cherbourg was 65 miles away Hitchens set course for there and, lying off, awaited the enemy's return. From later reports it seemed there were two groups of E-boats out that night both heading on a southerly course. Then a different report came. The E-boats had turned back - probably because of the fog. The gunboats sped on, towards Cherbourg, the fog cleared and it became a clear still night. As the MGBs closed to within 3 miles of Cherbourg the harbour navigation lights, obviously ordered for the E-boats return, came on. The MGBs cut their engines and in the sudden silence they heard *"a subdued rumble like the residue of a long drawn-out and slowly dying thunderclap"* which meant the E-boats must be about to enter the harbour. The signals had clearly indicated two groups of E-boats. Hitchens waited quietly about a mile off the entrance to the harbour in expectation of the arrival of the second group and shortly they were rewarded by the rumble of engines indicating the arrival of the second group slowing down to enter harbour. Hitchens spotted four in line ahead scarcely moving and presumably awaiting permission to enter. He led his gunboats quietly in astern of the enemy and beginning with the rear boat moved slowly up the line raking each in turn with devastating fire. The Germans were taken completely by surprise. It was about 10 minutes before the shore batteries and a couple of destroyers anchored off the breakwater realised what was happening and opened fire lightening the scene with starshell and 4" shells. The MGBs did enormous damage to the E-boats by circling in a tight line ahead formation at 24 knots firing into them with their new Rolls two-pounder guns. For 12 minutes Hitchens had dominated the battle but the time had come to make a getaway and he took it. As so often happened on these taken-by-surprise situations the enemy doesn't realise when the attacking force departs and the shooting still goes on amongst themselves as it did on this occasion. The MGBs paused about four miles in the friendly dark to count the cost which was remarkably light with only two casualties and a few holes in the boats. Looking back they saw two pillars of fire indicating a couple of E-boats were burning furiously.

Meeting up with Robert Hitchens and his officers on board BROCKLESBY in Dartmouth we heard of this brilliant battle in some detail and I was honoured to have the opportunity to meet this legendary figure. He was killed in action on 13th August 1943.

This torching of the Cherbourg E-boats seemed to have discouraged them from further cross-Channel sorties against our PW/WP convoys, although they remained based on Cherbourg and were to be met escorting the German coastal convoys. They, of course, caused us problems during the raid on Dieppe which was to take place in the near future.

Chapter X

THE DIEPPE RAID
19 August 1942

The global scene at July/August 1942 was extremely grim on many fronts; Winston Churchill aptly described this period 'The Hinge of Fate' when our fortunes went from almost uninterrupted disasters to almost consistent success. But it had to be earned the hard way.

On the naval front, which of course was of the greatest interest and significance to us, there was the disastrous raid on Dieppe in which BROCKLESBY was directly involved and lucky to survive. The U-boat offensive in the Atlantic and, particularly in American waters where they operated almost unchallenged until the US organised a convoy system, nearly forced the Allies to restrict the passage of convoys to and from Britain. Fortunately Hitler vetoed the deployment of the German Navy's heavy ships - battle cruisers, pocket battleships and cruisers - into the Atlantic as this could have been the last straw in succeeding to sever the lifeline of oil and war supplies for our hard pressed armies in North Africa and other vital theatres of war. Rommel was still rampant in the Desert and it wasn't until November 1942 that the great joint Anglo-American landing in North Africa code-named Operation TORCH and the Army's breakthrough at El Alamein signalled the turning of the 'Hinge of Fate' in our favour.

My affairs, of somewhat lesser importance, enabled me to book myself into Barrow Gurney hospital to have my increasingly painful damaged coccyx dealt with. There I met my old friend Alan Wills from HMT DUNERA days, who had been mine-sweeping around Singapore since the beginning of the war; he had had a dreary and boring time until chased out by the Japanese.

In their leisurely time the medics, Surg-Capts Oldham and Murray, took me in hand and made me sweat with pain by sticking needles in my spine. In front of the nurses they formally objected to me having a bottle of whisky in my bedside locker but didn't refuse a nip when they dropped in alone on their rounds. I was discharged on 15th July for a week's leave to recover and headed for Glasgow which took a particularly uncomfortable 24 hours on the train. During the latter part of July I was back in Barrow Gurney hospital a bit worried that my injured coccyx wasn't showing much improvement and might become a permanent handicap. Gradually however the pain eased and I decided I was going to live, so much so that in company with some walking wounded we broke out through the 'looney-bin' wire-fencing and visited the village pub for some excellent draught cider, known as 'Scrumpy'.

On 1st August I was back on board BROCKLESBY with a convoy to Milford Haven. On the return trip we went into Dartmouth and with the SGBs were off at dusk to sweep for E-boats off the Cherbourg Peninsula, returning to Plymouth at 0200 having had no contact.

At the Portsmouth end of our convoy beat I was able to meet up with Kenneth from time to time and have him aboard for dinner - he had now acquired a splendid 3-litre MG, the forerunner of a lifelong addiction to fast cars and events such as the Monte Carlo Rally.

Early in August we resumed a mixture of routine convoy duty and sorties out of Dartmouth with the MTBs over to the French coast in the hope of finding the E-boats putting to sea. These sweeps were not haphazard but based on intelligence reports.

All the evidence of 'something afoot' was picking up whenever we put into Portsmouth at the east end of our convoy run. There was not only visual confirmation of what was then strange looking landing craft and Infantry Assault Ships piling up in the harbour but at least one alert in late July of a big raid to the French coast involving, in particular, the mass of Canadian troops of the First Canadian Army who were roaming around Portsmouth and Southampton. Our sailors after a 'run ashore' to the pubs could tell us the latest state of play which with hindsight was accurate. The generally accepted target was Dieppe and it is surprising German intelligence had no forewarning.

On 12th August Nigel Pumphrey was summoned to Portsmouth

Combined Headquarters for a briefing. He returned to BROCKLESBY with our orders including photographs and charts with which he briefed myself and the navigator, Alistair Gilchrist. Our station was, in company with the Polish-manned Hunt Class destroyer SLAZAK, to protect the east flank of the assault force from enemy attack. I remember during our discussions on tactics with the CO of SLAZAK that in view of the lax security ashore and confirmation of Dieppe as the target we should expect strong opposition.

The code-name for the operation was JUBILEE. The preparatory signal was postponed one day to 17th August when 'standby' was received followed by the executive signal on the 18th which meant the fleet would sail that evening. It was a day of intense preparation, shipping extra ammunition stowed on deck, and checking that everything was in order for a calculated offensive - a different mental approach to my previous two years of warfare when action or reaction happened, it might be said, 'on the hoof'.

I 'cleared lower deck' at 1845 and the Captain told the crew of our objective which only confirmed what they knew already!

Having taken an active part in this operation I have researched the background and established it was approved by the Cabinet and Chiefs of Staff in April and delegated to the Chief of Combined Operations, Admiral Mountbatten, for execution. At this time there was stationed in Britain a large number of troops, especially Canadians, who had come from overseas to fight the Germans, for whom extended training and idleness was affecting morale. It was decided to use these troops amounting to 4961 officers and men as the spearhead of the force together with 1057 men of Nos 3 and 4 (Lord Lovat's) Commandos and the Royal Marine Commandos with a small number of United States Rangers. The Canadian battalions were the South Saskatchewan Regiment, Royal Regiment of Canada, Royal Hamilton Light Infantry, Canadian Essex Scottish, Cameron Highlanders of Canada and the Fusiliers Mount Royal.

These troops were carried in the Landing Ships Infantry (LSIs), a fleet of fast cross Channel and North Sea ferries converted to carry smaller specially developed troop and tank landing craft which were on davits and launched with their men and equipment as the LSIs approached the beaches. Other landing craft carried the Commandos and Rangers for the attacks on the gun batteries that protected the harbour about 5 miles east and west of Dieppe. All these landing ships and craft were assembled in Portsmouth, Southampton, Newhaven and Shoreham for embarkation rather like a miniature D-Day of the future.

It was a quiet evening on the 18th as, with a light south-west wind, we slipped and sailed in the twilight. The routine evening Jerry reconnaissance plane had flown over the harbour about half an hour before and surprisingly, according to post-war records, did not report anything unusual in Portsmouth or the Solent.

Together with the Polish Hunt Class destroyer SLAZAK, commanded by Captain Rommald Tyminski, who was the Senior Officer of our duo, we made for Spithead and according to plan were the last through the gate in the boom. Two flotillas of minesweepers had sailed at noon to clear and make a safe passage south through the Channel minefield. The main force, led by the Hunt Class destroyer CALPE, as Headquarters ship, with the calm night closing in and the moon in a clear sky, sailed to the east off Newhaven before turning south through the now swept channel towards France. The speed of the advance was about 15 knots dictated by the sea-keeping limits of the smaller landing craft. As the fleet cleared the exit of the swept channel about 10 miles off the French coast, it split and moved towards the several target beaches to the east and west of Dieppe. By midnight the moon had set but with the sky clear it was not particularly dark and it wasn't difficult to keep station on the troop ships and the landing craft. I was on the bridge with the Captain who always maintained he couldn't see properly at night, which was true, and he relied greatly on myself with my trusty Zeiss 7x50's and others to keep him posted. We were of course keeping radar and ASDIC watch – the latter's persistent 'ping' cut into the unusually tense atmosphere and the murmorous background noise of the engine room fans and the ship's ventilation system.

Together with SLAZAK we made towards the east to guard the

left flank of the craft carrying No 3 Commando which were being led into YELLOW Beaches No 1 and No 2 by SGB 5 at the head with ML 346 and a flak landing ship for protection at the rear. Col Dunford-Slater was commanding No 3 Commando and Cdr Wyburg RN was in command of the naval craft; both were aboard SGB 5. At 0330 SLAZAK and ourselves increased speed breaking away to the east to sweep the extreme left flank of the fleet as ordered in our instructions. And then a sequence of events and confusion struck our sector of the raid which led to a calamitous effect on the whole operation.

Quite early in the evening the British radar station at Dover had detected a group of five German vessels leaving Boulogne and heading south-westwards; presumably a convoy protected by escorts. When the dots from this convoy faded from the radar screen at Dover at about midnight, Portsmouth radar took over and at 0127 and again at 0244 signals were sent to CALPE, the headquarters Hunt, to alert the force commanders. These signals were not received by CALPE. However the second one was received by FERNIE, but they assumed CALPE had received it and taken action to alert SLAZAK and BROCKLESBY. Presumably due to the mandatory wireless silence, we heard nothing from CALPE, nor directly from Portsmouth radar station as our radio operators were tuned to the Force communication channels. Thus the disaster developed.

From post-war records this German convoy from Boulogne consisted of five commandeered Dutch schutjes (coastal motor vessels) escorted by an armed minesweeper and two submarine chasers of the German Navy. Their destination was Dieppe with a scheduled arrival time of 0500. One submarine chaser was leading the convoy, with the other one astern and the armed minesweeper well to seaward to give a clear field of fire against the ever-present threat of marauding British gunboats along this stretch of the coast.

No-one seems to know what exactly happened at 0345. On our radar we had had the blips of No 3 Commando's landing craft on our radar screen, now some seven miles away. They were heading for Berneval to land on the two YELLOW Beaches, with the objective to destroy the 5.9cm heavy gun battery protecting the eastern approaches to Dieppe about four miles to the west.

This group, which had left directly from Newhaven, originally consisted of 23 landing craft personnel (LCPs), and one landing craft flak (LCF), lightly protected by SGB 5 and ML 346. The LCPs, scow-like craft named 'Eurekas' made of plywood, were capable of carrying about 20 men; they would never have stood up to the Channel crossing had the sea been rough. As it was, four of these boats had to return to Newhaven with engine trouble and the remaining 19, with a speed of about 9 $^1/_2$ knots, were formed up behind SGB 5 which had aboard Col Durnford-Slater, the CO of No 3 Commando, together with the fifty US Rangers. Cdr Wyburg was also on board SGB 5 as the naval officer in charge of Group 5, all the craft now heading for the YELLOW Beaches. ML 346 and the flak landing craft were now in station at the rear.

At 0345 it was still dark, the moon having set and about 45 minutes to elapse to nautical twilight, when Cdr Wyburg on the bridge of SGB 5 spotted a dark shape on his port bow. This was followed immediately by blinding starshell from this group which revealed about five ships in an arc from port to starboard across his bows. This starshell was accompanied by heavy and accurate gunfire from the enemy which raked SGB 5 fore and aft, destroying her wireless aerials and killing several of her crew, which prevented her from alerting CALPE of the attack. Cdr Wyburg endeavoured to keep leading Group 5 which was now about seven miles from touchdown at Berneval. However SGB 5 was now in a shambles, capable of only about 6 knots and all her guns out of action. As I have commented earlier, these SGBs, designed as our answer to the German E-boats, whilst fast and well armed, had an Achilles heel. If one of the many high-pressure steam pipes from the Yarrow boilers powering the turbines was hit by even a small calibre shell, the vessel filled with super-heated steam and caused hideous casualties. Only one flotilla of these imaginative but fragile craft was ever built.

The LCF mounting two twin 4" guns came furiously into the fight, surprising the enemy and setting the leading submarine chaser, UJ 1404, on fire. UJ 1404 then blew up and was apparently lost with all hands. The other submarine chaser, UJ 4014, had been badly damaged by SGB 5 before she was put out of action, and together with UJ 1411 broke off the fight to return to their convoy of schutjes to shepherd it onward to Le Tréport.

We, of course, in SLAZAK and BROCKLESBY were on a sweep to the east progressively distancing ourselves from the fracas and tragically took no part in this battle which we decisively could have affected if we had received the warning signals from Portsmouth radar to CALPE. I often wonder why in SLAZAK or BROCKLESBY we did not receive this vital information directly. Although we were keeping watch on the dedicated radio links with CALPE, we could also have listened out on the CinC's usual Portsmouth waveband. We obviously did not.

Because of wireless silence our contact with SLAZAK was by dimmed Aldis lamp and when we saw the starshell arching to the south-west, Nigel Pumphrey, responding to the Nelsonian precept that you cannot do better than lay yourself alongside the enemy, immediately turned BROCKLESBY about and we started firing starshells towards the distant action. The senior officer, Capt Tyminski of SLAZAK, however ordered us to ceasefire and resume station still heading on a zigzag course to the east. This was a wrong decision as we would have been able to lend weight to the battle in progress or at least cut off the enemy convoy and escorts from reaching Le Tréport.

This unhappy circumstance of the well-armed German convoy slipping through our guard to collide undetected with the loaded landing craft an hour from the scheduled touchdown was a major setback which had a knock-on effect to the whole Dieppe raid. First, the YELLOW Beach landings were compromised and the vital element of surprise lost; second, the landing craft fleet were in disarray despite gallant efforts by Lt Fear RN in ML 346 who rounded them up as best he could, and led them towards YELLOW Beach One. Here, what was left of 3 Commando in five Eureka LCPs landed in daylight to meet a fully alerted enemy. Only one landing craft with about 20 commandos aboard had landed earlier unopposed on YELLOW Beach Two and between them harassed the heavy 5.9 cm Goebels battery, at least preventing the German gunners from shelling the invasion fleet. Their contribution without their leader, Col Durnford-Slater, was magnificent and heroic. Durnford-Slater and Cdr Wyburg, the naval force commander, had abandoned the wrecked SGB 5 and had taken to an LCP in an attempt to report, in the absence of a radio link, the situation to the Naval Force commander, Capt Hughes-Hallet (who, incidentally, had also been on the St Nazaire Raid) on CALPE. They didn't reach CALPE until nearly 0700 unaware that a substantial number of No 3 Commando had gathered themselves together after the collision with the German convoy and pressed on ashore. On this news Cdr Wyburg commandeered MGB 317 and returned to the YELLOW Beaches to see what he could do to help. By the time he reached there, the remnants of No 3 Commando had completed their attack and were withdrawing with their wounded being still supported by Lt Fear in ML 346.

On our part it wasn't long before Capt Tyminski in SLAZAK realised we were doing no good out on the wing so eventually we turned back to where the main landings were now in full fling. As scheduled the RAF appeared at dawn to take their part in the show.

It was now after 0500 and full daylight when we ran over what had been the scene of the action with the German convoy; there were no ships visible but swimming around in the water were 40 or so Germans who had been on the submarine chaser UJ 1404 sunk by the flak landing craft. We and SLAZAK fished these sailors, who were hanging onto bits of wreckage, out of the drink, locked them in the tiller flat and eventually landed them at Portsmouth.

Dieppe – The Main Assault

It was after dawn by the time we rescued the German seamen, our catch being 25, including one who was still wearing his steel helmet. I was keen to rescue him out of the water as I fancied his helmet as a souvenir, and to this day I have it hanging in my garage. SLAZAK had also picked up some Germans but for some reason had none to land when we returned to the UK.

We then set off to join the ships off Dieppe harbour where the main body of troops and tanks had hit the beach at 0510. At this moment the RAF arrived with a whoosh and lots of bangs and for the rest of the day the skies were a battle ground of their own over Dieppe. A total of 67 squadrons consisting of Spitfires, Hurricanes, Mustangs, Bostons and Blenheims were deployed, 47 of these were Spitfires which although good defensive planes did have not have much clout. Coastal Command had flown some anti-surface vessel patrols during the hours of darkness preceding the operation. I wish they had come our way perhaps to spot the armed enemy convoy which had so disrupted 3 Commando heading for YELLOW Beaches.

It was 0515 and full daylight when the first of the Spitfires escorting the 'Hurri-bombers' swept over to attack the gun emplacements along and around Dieppe Harbour; they met heavy anti-aircraft fire but at that time no opposition from German aircraft. It was nearly 0700 before FW 190s and ME 109s began appearing over Dieppe and from then on the skies over the town and the ships lying off were one continuous dogfight. I remember noting with awe this amazing scene as whichever way I looked there were parachutes, RAF and Luftwaffe, floating down gently onto the sea and the airmen of both sides being picked up by the patrolling Air Sea Rescue craft of the RAF.

The FW 190s, probably the best fighter flying at this stage of the war, had tremendous battles with the Spitfires and Hurricanes who were disadvantaged by their greater distance from base, flying as they were from UK airfields.

From our point of view and that of the Canadian troops and tanks struggling to land on the beaches, the most effective air support came from the three squadrons of smoke-laying Bostons and Blenheims. They were extremely brave, flying close and low along the coast and beaches in the face of sheets of anti-aircraft fire. Apart from the welcome cover the curtains of smoke gave to the exposed soldiers clawing their way up the beaches, it also enabled the ships to pop in and out of the layers of smoke distracting the enemy's shore batteries gunlayers from concentrating on any particular target, i.e. us!

The enemy had by 1000 alerted their bomber squadrons from as far away as Holland and soon JU 88s, Heinkel 111s and Dornier 217s arrived on the scene, appearing mainly to target the ships and landing-craft lying offshore. By this time of course the nine LSIs, such as HMS GLENGYLE, had dropped their landing-craft and gone off home; none of them having been damaged.

On our side the US Army Air Force (USAAF) fielded 24 Flying Fortresses which, escorted by four squadrons of Spitfires, bombed the airfield at Abbeville just east of Dieppe, closing it for hours and destroying three FW 190s on the ground. All the US planes returned safely to base.

In BROCKLESBY we were now under direct control of the headquarters ship CALPE and were ordered to support the Canadian battalions attempting to land on the beaches to the east of the main harbour. The total weight and strength of the fire of the eight Hunts' 4" guns and other support craft was not nearly sufficient to deal with the power and density of the defender's well entrenched 88s' and 75s' gun emplacements. As regards bombing the enemy gun positions prior to the raid, British policy was the same as in the earlier raid on St Nazaire, namely not to bomb French towns. A request by Admiral Mountbatten for a battleship had been turned down on the grounds that the risk of its exposure to bombs or mines was too great. The deployment of either or both of these options would have greatly increased the possibility of a successful raid and would have certainly mitigated the horrendous casualties.

HMS LOCUST, commanded by Cdr Robert Ryder VC who had led the raid on St Nazaire a few months before, was a shallow draft gunboat armed with two 4" guns. It led in the seven 150 ton Free French Chasseurs[26] carrying the Royal Marine Commandos and had been given the ambitious objective of 'cutting out' and capturing German

---

[26] Small French river gun-boats

invasion barges lying in Dieppe's inner harbour. LOCUST went in about 0600 but within ten minutes had been overpowered by heavy fire from the recesses of the 'Bismarck' battery on the eastern headland and rendered useless. She retired with the Commandos in the Chasseurs who were later transferred to landing craft and used as a last desperate card by the Force Commander at about 0830 to reinforce the troops that had landed on WHITE Beach. It was a futile gesture, making the fatal mistake of reinforcing failure, and the Marine Commandos suffered heavy casualties and achieved nothing.

Meantime we had earlier moved close into the beaches doing our best to make some impression on the strongly protected heavy gun emplacements marked on our plans, and the concrete pill-boxes along the cliffs from which an endless stream of cannon and machine-gun fire was raking the Canadian soldiers attempting to cross the beach onto the promenade. We had no visible effect on the big gun batteries but we seemed to have some success in silencing some of the pill-boxes and fortified houses along the clifftops. We were at the same time making smoke to protect the troops and tanks being landed, and to cover the landing craft carrying the wounded who were now making their way back to the bigger ships lying offshore: at the same time we wove in and out of the banks of smoke to avoid becoming a sitting target ourselves. As it was, we received a steady rain of small calibre shells which fortunately caused no casualties and did little damage.

However at about 0830 we received a signal from CALPE that ten E-boats had sailed from Boulogne to the east and were heading towards Dieppe and we, together with SLAZAK and BLEASDALE, were despatched east to intercept. This report turned out to be false and our departure at this critical time diminished the already inadequate fire support being brought to bear against the enemy guns in support of the men ashore. Returning to the fray we continued moving in and out of the banks of smoke about 500 yards offshore and were consistently being peppered by shells of sufficient calibre to pierce the hull and upperworks, continuing to avoid casualties and significant damage. By about 0900 the Military Force Commander had realised the game was up and it was decided to withdraw, but the momentous order was postponed as for some obscure reason it would have upset the RAF's protective smoke-laying timetable.

The scene on the narrow beaches, which I could see as the curtains of smoke ebbed and flowed, was quite horrendous to the point of being unbelievable. There was little if any movement amongst the men ashore, many of whom were dead or wounded; hundreds and hundreds being thickly sprawled in a grotesque tangle quite thick up the beaches to the line of cliffs. Snipers were picking off any that did move. We kept up the firing as best we could to cover the withdrawal while the landing-craft were sent in to rescue the troops, but they in turn became targets for the enemy. I witnessed ghastly scenes of survivors ashore rushing the ramps which then became clogged with dead and wounded.

So far we in BROCKLESBY had been lucky, with Mort Duffus, himself a Canadian, in charge of the Director Control Tower spotting our targets and continuously firing salvos to the best advantage. But the nut was too hard to crack and our relatively feeble firepower had little impact. The withdrawal was distressingly protracted; it seemed a dreadfully slow operation and there was no let up in the enemy's reaction. In fact with the arrival of more and more enemy aircraft, the attacks on our ships lying close offshore increased the intensity. Our Pom-Poms and Oerlikons were constantly in action.

At 1130 Nigel Pumphrey moved closer inshore, the better to improve our covering fire, but this nearly brought disaster when we grounded on a sandbank and stuck fast about 400 yards off the beach. As we were now a much easier target than a moving vessel, the guns ashore concentrated on us between the gaps in the smoke screen. Heavy shells crashed aboard. We were a trophy for the guns ashore, it wouldn't be long before we were battered to pieces. Both engines were put out of action for about five minutes and when restarted the Captain and Lt(E) Albert Lee wrestled to free us which thankfully they did. However the thrashing around put the port gearbox and propeller out of action with a bent tail-shaft. We were thus reduced to half power with only one propeller operating: this did not help.

At this fraught moment I was distracted by the crash of a heavy shell aft on the quarterdeck, and as I moved along the deck to see what damage might have been done, the quarterdeck 4" gun crew came flying past me. When I reached the point where the shell had landed, I found it had split open the cartridge cases of several of the 4" ready-use shells in their lockers and sticks of burning cordite were fizzing about the deck. Fortunately at that moment the Gunner (T), Walter Betts, also arrived on the scene and with great presence of mind helped by his training and experience with explosives, we together started to kick the shells and cordite over the side. The twin 4" gun mounting was twisted and the guns no longer functioned. The German prisoners in the tiller flat below must have thought the end was nigh. Most surprisingly none of the gun's crew were injured.

BROCKLESBY shook and shuddered as full power was turned on our remaining screw, and the good ship gradually dug herself out of the sandbank and we were free and relatively safe.

We had been observing and helping with one of the few minor successes of those troops who had managed to landed. A prominent building ashore was the three storied Casino which had a heavy gun emplacement on its seaward side. Its guns had been firing directly onto the troops and tanks landing on the beaches below. This was stormed by the Royal Hamilton Light Infantry who eventually broke in and silenced the guns. A few of the tanks actually made it from the shingle beach onto the promenade and from there a little way into the town, but the attack was soon stalled by the Germans and it petered out. This building had been one of our targets.

Although we were limping along on one screw, we still remained fairly close in to the beaches and continued to fire at targets ashore with our for'd 4" mounting. We were also able to provide anti-aircraft fire to give protection to the troops and the landing craft which were now beginning to evacuate the Canadians. All this time our scrambling nets were draped over the side to help the many soldiers swimming about in the water to come aboard. Most needed assistance as they were weighed down by wet clothing and, despite the rain of small calibre shot and shell, our crew went over the side to help them aboard. We gathered a total of 80 Canadians who were taken below to the wardroom, petty officers' messes, and cabins. The wounded were treated in the sick-bay by Doc Healey with his SBAs[27] who did great work. Our sailors with their usual generosity did a wonderful job comforting these shocked men. Navy rum and spirits from the wardroom did wonders.

The Return Home

Shortly after 1300, when the final withdrawal was ordered and we had just joined the retreating fleet, a JU 88 being pursued by our fighters jettisoned a heavy bomb as she passed over BERKELEY. It landed on the bridge, killing the Captain, Lt Yorke RN, and broke the back of the ship which then had to be sunk by a torpedo from ALBRIGHTON after the crew had been rescued by her and Peter Scott's SGB 8. The 200 ships and landing craft full of wounded mustered together to provide concentrated anti-aircraft protection for the journey home.

The RAF had been looking forward to their involvement in the raid to have a showdown with the Luftwaffe, but whilst they gave marvellous protection with their smoke laying and bombing, the final score was heavily in favour of the opposition. We lost a total of 106 aircraft, 88 of them Spitfires, and the enemy only 47. The RAF had flown 2617 sorties and in my view their performance that day was magnificent.

The remainder of the journey back across the Channel was harried by FW 190s and JU 88s, but little damage was sustained apart from a hit on CALPE. Running on one engine, with the aid of tugs we berthed in Portsmouth about 0200 with SLAZAK alongside. Ambulances were waiting on the dockside. We landed our own fatal casualty, Able Seaman Richardson, and our five wounded and the 80 Canadian survivors, many of whom were also wounded and heavily shocked. It was nearly noon

---

[27] Sick-Bay Attendants.

before the Army came aboard to relieve us of our 25 German prisoners. I then took the Army major over to SLAZAK to introduce him to my opposite number and casually asked him if he had any trouble with his prisoners which I had seen being picked up from the sea. He replied *"Prisoners – what prisoners?"* From this I deduced that the Poles really did not like the Hun.

An abiding regret I have about the raid was the almost exclusive use of Canadian forces for the main assault on the beaches. Their numbers were not great; about 5000 in total although a disproportionate 3500 were killed, captured or wounded, but this day in Canada has become revered and remembered like Gallipoli of the First War has been for Australia and New Zealand. If the main force had been a mixed one with British or other troops, the criticism of the Canadian sacrifice would have had little foundation. As it was the Navy, RAF and Commandos also paid a huge price. In retrospect there were two aspects of that fatal day which could perhaps have turned defeat into victory; one would have been a heavy bombing raid on the defences and the other to have had a battleship on station for a limited period to achieve the same. It is interesting to note that Winston Churchill had been a major figure in the decision to mount both the Gallipoli and Dieppe operations.

We went into dock the following day and made a survey of the damage sustained: eight shell holes of around 3 inch calibre plus some 200 holes from shrapnel and smaller calibre shells, fortunately all of them above the waterline. An unexploded 88mm shell was found underneath the main generator in the engine room. The Admiralty for some unexplained reason sent down the well known physicist (and communist), Professor J B Bernal, to prepare a report on this damage; this report I never saw. The bad news was that, as we would be hors de combat for some weeks, our superb Captain, Nigel Pumphrey, was to be whipped out and appointed to another Hunt, HMS GOATHLAND. This called for a farewell party and then he was gone but we remained friends from then on. He was awarded a bar to his DSO in the Dieppe Honours List, and our Chief Engineer, Lt(E) Albert Lee RN, received a

DSC. I then sent most of the crew off on leave and as soon as I had organised the repair programme with the Dockyard, I pushed off on leave myself to join Kirsteen who was holidaying at West Kilbride with Sheena Dundas and our children.

With the country still buzzing over the raid and the propaganda machine trying to make the best of it here and in Canada, it was lovely and peaceful with beautiful weather on the Ayrshire coast. Willis Roxburgh, now back from pilot training in Rhodesia, had been posted to Coastal Command and was based in Benbecula, of all places, as captain of a Flying Fortress. He came down to West Kilbride for the night and we had a round of golf just like old times.

I had to return to BROCKLESBY to attend to the changeover of watches returning and going on leave and to check on the progress of the damage repairs, as well as to confer with the new Captain, Lt Cdr Blackler RN – I didn't go much on him. Eventually, however, I had a decent spell of leave as repairs dragged on, but during this time my father, Kirsteen and I had a fun visit to London over 22nd/23rd September for an investiture at Buckingham Palace by King George VI where he presented me with my DSC. The previous night we stayed in the Old Berkeley Hotel in Piccadilly with its Hatchett's Restaurant and dance band below. The next morning Dad had a quiet chortle with his instruction to the taxi-driver *"Buckingham Palace, please."*[28] When confronting the King on the dais I was taken aback by the amount of quite thick make-up he had on! Nigel Pumphrey and his wife, Frances, were also there that day, he to pick up his second DSO for Dieppe. We went off and had a merry lunch afterwards.

Unfortunately I had to return to the ship at Portsmouth but soon took off on leave again until early October when, after a working up period, we resumed our convoy escort routine in the western Channel.

---

[28] This scene was re-enacted on 1 December 1992, exactly 50 years later, when I accompanied my son, AK, and his wife Carol to Buckingham Palace when he received his OBE. The taxi was directed in the same words and with a similar chortle.

On 13th October we had a punch up off the Channel Islands with a group of other Hunts when the commerce raider KOMET was blown up and sunk, the story of which I have recounted earlier in this book. By this time I was getting fed up with the captain, Lt Cdr Blackler, particularly following another sortie to the French Coast when we engaged six German ships near Les Sept Isles and then withdrew after a desultory attack which we should have pressed home. Blackler was carpeted by the CinC, Admiral Charles Forbes, and I thought he might lose his job[29]. However, I received a call from Forbes' Secretary that evening of 2nd November to say a relief for me was on the way. As it turned out the Captain side-tracked this RN Lieutenant and managed to appoint Mort Duffus to the job. Mort had earned it and was entirely competent. After a rough passage round Land's End to Milford Haven in weather so bad we couldn't run liberty boats in harbour, I said goodbye to my chums in BROCKLESBY and went ashore at dawn on 7th November from where I had joined her 17 months before.

The journey north was one of the worst ever, taking over 27 hours; eight of them spent overnight on Crewe Station with a hangover. This slow parting with the happy ship BROCKLESBY gave me plenty of time to reminisce on the good and the bad times with nothing to regret and much to be thankful for. By early 1943 BROCKLESBY had left Plymouth Command for the Mediterranean where she spent the next two years on very active service. Although she was one of the earliest Hunts to be built (in Cammell Lairds), she was the last of the class to be decommissioned in 1963 after 22 years' service.

---

[29] Later in the month, on 19th November, after Blackler had, as senior officer of the escort, mishandled the protection of his convoy in another confrontation with E-boats near the Eddystone Lighthouse, there was a Court of Enquiry on the incident.

Chapter XI

HMS GRIFFIN
CONVOY TACTICS AT DERBY HOUSE
November 1942 – 10 April 1943

L ater in the month of November I made a sortie to London and the Admiralty in an attempt to influence my next appointment; as it was likely to be as a First Lieutenant on a Fleet destroyer, I was going to try for a stand-by job on a new destroyer building on the Clyde. Leave drifted on happily covering Susanne's first birthday party on 27th November, but the next day my appointment came through to HMS GRIFFIN, a 'G' Class Fleet destroyer refitting at Thornycroft's yard at Southampton, of all wartime dreary and battered places. Before joining her I attended a Damage Control Course in Colet Gardens, London which was interesting and had short hours of attendance enabling me to indulge in some social life on the Town – despite air raid restrictions there were plenty of cinemas, concerts and theatres to enjoy: the Albert Hall had regular weekly concerts free to anyone in uniform. Brother Kenneth turned up in London having missed a passage to America due to a cock-up in the Admiralty and we met up with an old friend, Ralph Dundas, also in London for some reason – so you see there were many contacts in the Metropolis. Kenneth headed for Liverpool, there to await passage for America to take up his appointment as Gunnery Officer on the cruiser EURYALUS which was being repaired in a Brooklyn yard. After a few days back home I eventually joined GRIFFIN on 7th December and met the Captain, Lt Cdr Tony Rowell, who turned out to be an unpleasant character. I took over from Lt J A J Dennis RN who gave me the low-down on Rowell and was glad to be moving on. I stayed in the bomb battered and run down Royal Hotel where I had previously lodged when refitting BROCKLESBY.

The refit of GRIFFIN dragged on with the ship getting ever more dirty and sordid, and I managed to escape back to our new home at

Arnwood Drive for Christmas where we had a happy party with the Orrs up from Ayr and Dad around. Helen Fergusson (Kilpatrick) came in with the news that Hunter Roxburgh had been killed on his Hunt in the Mediterranean. I saw a very grieved Willis that evening. I returned to Southampton where I divided my time between GRIFFIN and attending a Destroyer Gunnery Officer's course at Whale Island where I met a fun group of No 1s of all the latest Fleet destroyers. Our instructor was an RN Gunnery Officer, Lt Begg, who had been a contemporary of mine at Kelvinside Academy. Connected in some way with 'Whaley' was Admiral Bell-Davies VC who lived at Lee-on-Solent and was renowned for the parties he staged; on Hogmanay 1942 he had a huge fancy-dress party which I 'first-footed' in traditional Scottish fashion and spent the night, returning to 'Whaley' by bus the next morning. Mort Duffus phoned from Portsmouth where BROCKLESBY had come in for a couple of hours so I ran down to see my old shipmates and collect my motorbike which they had kept on board: I have no record of what happened to it thereafter.

January 1943 and the refit to GRIFFIN dragged on. Kirsteen managed a few days in London where again we stayed in our favourite hotel, the original Berkeley, had supper at Pruniers and a visit to the Windmill Theatre, also famous for its hoofers[30] and motto *"We never closed"*: a reference to its record of never closing however bad the blitz and bombs. The following night we had some dinner and danced our tune *'The Lady is a Tramp'* to Geraldo's band at the Savoy after seeing *'The Man who came to Dinner'* at the Savoy Theatre. I had been ordered on an Anti-Submarine (A/S) Tactical Course at the nerve centre of our anti-submarine campaign based at Western Approaches Headquarters at Derby House in Liverpool. So on the Sunday, 24th January, Kirsteen and I left London for Liverpool staying at the Adelphi, which I noted in my diary as a 'poor hotel now': its reputation doesn't seem to have improved in 50 years. She went on to Glasgow on the Monday and I started the A/S course which was fascinating, particularly

---

[30] Chorus line.

the plot in Derby House where all our Atlantic convoys and the attendant U-boats were constantly displayed and updated night and day on huge screens and tables by groups of Wrens. At this point in time the battle of the Atlantic was reaching its most furious and potentially serious climax with the U-boat wolf-packs being masterminded by Dönitz now Commander-in-Chief of the German Navy; he having succeeded Admiral Raeder who had fallen out with Hitler. The experienced submariner, Admiral Sir Max Horton, was CinC of Western Approaches Command based at Derby House.

During these visits to Derby House we avidly learnt about the ever-developing tactics of our Escort Groups and the latest weapon technology. Coastal Command had at last been allocated sufficient long-range aircraft and, in co-operation with the US Air Force, were now able to cover the 'Greenland air gap' with anti-U-boat patrols over all the Atlantic. The innovative Leigh lights now being fitted to those aircraft together with centimetre radar were proving effective at catching U-boats on the surface at night.

Apart from being briefed about the latest equipment, such as the forward firing 'Hedgehog' mortar bombs, and HF/DF to intercept U-boat transmissions and pinpoint their positions directly from our escorts, the main thrust of our lectures from a team headed by the renowned Capt Gilbert Roberts was the tactics which had been painstakingly developed (and I mean that) by Capt 'Johnnie' Walker, Peter Gretton and others in their destroyer, frigate and corvette escort groups. The box search for a U-boat lying 'doggo' at depth, and Walker's most effective tactic of one stopped escort holding a U-boat in her ASDIC beam whilst another crossed at right angles and then signalled when to drop her depth charges were two absorbing gems of experience which we were fortunate to assimilate on this course. We were also made aware of the perilous threat to the Atlantic convoys as the U-boats closed the American coastline where they were operating having a second 'happy time' against poorly escorted coastal convoys. During the time I was on the course in January 1943 it was estimated that there were 100 U-boats on station in the north and central Atlantic and the great battle upon which Britain's survival depended was about to begin. Dönitz now had a free hand with all the resources of the Kriegsmarine at his command and he was going to demonstrate his long held contention that severing our sea-borne lifeline was the path to victory.

It was clear to all of us on the course that the fortitude and morale of the seamen manning the allied merchant ships and tankers, who were almost powerless to defend themselves directly was a vital factor in this long battle. My admiration for these Merchant Navy officers and seamen on these Atlantic convoys and the onward routing to Russia is not exceeded by any other body of men in this war.

After the war it was established that the enemy had long been able to de-cypher our convoy control signals and it was not until May 1943 that our codes were changed to a more secure system. Meanwhile the reading by German intelligence of the tactical alterations of course signalled to Convoy Commodores by the Admiralty to avoid U-boat concentrations was useful information allowing Dönitz to deploy his wolf-packs to advantage. To us on the course this concentration of learning and advice had enormous impact – at least it did to me – as we were all heading for appointments on ships engaged in this fearsome battle.

Statistics of the Battle of the Atlantic during the time I was on the course record that a lightly escorted convoy of nine tankers from Trinidad to Gibraltar carrying fuel for our operations in the Mediterranean was attacked and only two survived. Another slow convoy from America to the UK, SC 118, consisting of sixty-three ships and ten escorts was attacked by about 20 U-boats and lost thirteen ships. Three U-boats were sunk and two were seriously damaged by the escorts. Altogether in February 1943 U-boats accounted for sixty-three ships and their score shot up to one hundred and eighty in March, a total of over 600,000 tons; this despite the air-cover and odd escort carrier accompanying our support groups now being available.

Chapter XII

HMS ORWELL
ATLANTIC AND RUSSIAN CONVOYS
10 April – 19 December 1943

I took a fortnight's leave after the A/S Tactical Course but eventually drifted back to Southampton to see how GRIFFIN was progressing. It had been the most protracted refit imaginable with the work force showing no sign of urgency; they begged the question *"Do you know there's a war on?"*. Over the next few weeks we approached completion of the refit and modernisation of the ship, which included the latest radar, 'Arcticisation' for the cold Russian run, and another ex-QUEEN MARY mattress for my cabin. The officer complement arrived in dribs and drabs including the captain, Lt Cdr Tony Rowell, who fortunately didn't hang around too much. Towards the end of February a rumour started circulating that GRIFFIN was to be handed over to an 'ally' as yet unspecified. This was later confirmed to be the Canadians so after all the dreary work on GRIFFIN I was back on the market.

Unfortunately as No 1 I had to remain with GRIFFIN until the Canadian complement of very raw officers and men arrived from their barracks at Greenock, and I even sailed on trials with them before handing over. There was a naming ceremony when her name was changed to HMCS OTTAWA[31]; after the accompanying party I pushed off on leave once again. Eventually the telegram arrived to report to the Captain of the Base at Hull, of all places. On 10th April 1943 I joined HMS ORWELL of the 17th DF and immediately started to take over from Lt H J Lee DSC who made off as quickly as he decently could! I also met the captain, Lt Cdr John Hodges DSO who also was heading for leave, so I had time to find my feet aboard my new ship.

---

[31] Her predecessor bearing the same name had been sunk in September 1942.

Louis Miller, the author's father, Kirsteen and the
author following his investiture by King George VI
outside Buckingham Palace 22nd September 1942

The author and 'Scrym' Scrymgeour-Wedderburn aboard HMS *Orwell*

HMS Orwell's Football Team 1942
Back Row: Arthur Percy (far right)
Middle Row: CPO Colston, Lt Alan Miller RNVR (1st Lt), Lt Cdr John Hodges DSO RN (Captain), Sub Lt Binch RNVR.
Front Row: AB Sid Godden, Mr Blackburn (NAAFI), NK, NK, AB Tommy Lodge

U-boat Captain, Oberleutnant Spiedal, and members of his crew being landed at Greenock from *HMS Orwell* on 10th Oct 1943 following their capture after attacks on convoy ONS 19 when the Polish-manned Fleet Destroyer *Orkan* was sunk. The author sees them off to POW camp.

She was one of our latest Fleet destroyers of the 'O' Class then based on Scapa Flow and employed on Arctic convoy duties to Murmansk. When not so engaged she acted as a member of the 3rd Escort Group in the North Atlantic backing up the escorts when the U-boat wolf-packs fell on the convoys.

My new captain, John Hodges, had not long been in command of the recently commissioned ORWELL having previously commanded the destroyer ANTHONY during the capture of Diego Saurez, the main port of Madagascar which owed allegiance to the Vichy Government. The operation was aimed at denying the island to the advancing Japanese to maintain our access to the Red Sea and the Middle East. In a brilliant exercise of ship-handling, when the landing forces were held up by the defences of the capital, Antsirane, he took ANTHONY in with a small party of Royal Marines and landed them in the enemy's rear having made a skilful 'stern board' to the quay in a strong offshore wind. This was the key to the collapse of all Vichy resistance on the island and was the action for which John Hodges was awarded the DSO.

ORWELL was in dry dock in the hands of Amos & Smith in Hull for a scrub and a short refit which is always a state of disruption, with officers and men coming and going on leave. I nipped back home for the weekend – Hull being much handier than Devonport – but was back on board for a very quiet birthday on 21st April celebrated with a phone call from Kirsteen and a glass of port! There was a tragic accident a few days later when a young sailor, Ordinary Seaman Papworth, who was on guard duty on the inward end of the 'brow',[32] must have been playing around with his revolver when it went off and he shot himself under his chin. I rushed up from my cabin, and with the duty sick-bay attendant, did what we could to resuscitate him but he died in the ambulance on the way to hospital. As we were in dock, on dry land so to speak, I wasn't sure where jurisdiction lay so I called the Police and an Inspector and his sidekick came down aboard. We discussed the situation and I laid on a few drinks for everyone's benefit. It was late

---

[32] gangway

and a dark, wet night by the time I saw the policemen over the side: the Inspector lost his footing as he stepped off the brow and he fell into the dry dock, which was empty of water, crashing down terrace after terrace until coming to a stop near the bottom; more ambulances were called and the poor fellow spent months in hospital with awful injuries. A night not easily forgotten and here recounted.

Kirsteen came down to Hull for a few days where we stayed in the comfortable Station Hotel dining there with John Hodges and coming on board for lunch to meet my new messmates. One of them, Lt Paddy Satow RN, our navigator, had recently been married to Mary Bergius whom we both knew. I went north with Kirsteen and Paddy for a few days leave then back to the ship with everyone returned from leave and preparing for sea. As we left the William Wright dry-dock on 9th May to do a tilt test we bumped the wall and had to go back in for a check up! At last on 11th May we turned left at the entrance to the Humber and made for Scapa at 2100 carrying out full power trials on the way in a howling gale. After a day in Scapa we were off to sea for a night exercise screening the battleship VALIANT and the cruiser GLASGOW, an old friend from the southern oceans, with Cargill Sandeman on board. Other A/S and HA[33] shoot exercises with INGLEFIELD and CHANTICLEER followed. We then departed on a zigzag passage to Gibraltar screening the battleship HOWE in company with ONSLOW and INGLEFIELD, taking a course to the west of Ireland. The weather improved as we passed Portugal and altered course for the Straits. A signal was intercepted indicating BROCKLESBY was also making for Gib, the start of her Mediterranean career. As we were only to be in harbour for the afternoon and evening of 25th May, I went aboard BROCKLESBY and had dinner with my old chums – Mort Duffus, Gilchrist, etc. Blackler was still in command which wasn't good news.

Although ORWELL of the 17th DF was of modern design, completed and commissioned in 1942, of 1600 tons displacement, 40,000 HP with a speed of 35 knots, there was one useful feature enjoyed

---

[33] High Angle

by the Hunt Class, from which I had recently come, which had not yet been introduced to the Fleet destroyers now building. This was the arrangement of the accommodation whereby the Officers' and Petty Officers' quarters were situated beneath the bridge and the crews quarters were fore and aft close under their action stations. This enabled everyone to reach their posts more quickly and safely, especially in the wild conditions of the North Atlantic and Arctic Ocean. All Fleet destroyers of the 'R' Class and later had the improved layout.

Sea conditions on the Atlantic and Russian convoy routes often required lifelines or jack-stays to be rigged along the upper deck when the seas swept aboard in bad weather and it was sometimes necessary to bring the ship head to wind whilst the watch was being changed. This was done as quickly as possible by command over the Tannoy. The captain had his sea cabin below the bridge which was always used at sea. The other officers' cabins in ORWELL were right aft which in wild conditions meant a difficult and hazardous journey to the bridge when the 'Action Stations' alarm was pressed.

We sailed from Gibraltar that night at 2330 on the 25th to escort the battleship NELSON to Devonport. It was a slow passage at 15 knots as she had been damaged whilst operating with Force 'H' in support of the North African campaign. On arriving in Plymouth on 30th May it was fun to be back in these familiar waters where we went to the same old oiler and called on more or less the same old staff in Captain 'D''s office. It was a lovely day which reminded me of our honeymoon exactly three years before. I managed to put a call through to Kirsteen. After a day in Devonport we sailed independently at 2000 for the Clyde where we picked up WARSPITE on 1st June and screened her to Scapa.

Following a couple of exhausting days sitting on a passing-out board for Petty Officers and Leading Seamen, plus dining a party from the new flotilla leader, GRENVILLE of the 'U' Class on which Kenneth was later to be the flotilla 'G' or Gunnery Officer, we sailed on 4th June at 2000 for Akuyreri in the north of Iceland with mail and some passengers. Akuyreri is at the head of a fjord which served as an assembly port for escorts for the Russian convoys and an oiler was permanently based there. The name rhymes with Tipperary and it's also a long way to go! It was quite a large town where 'goodies' such as tweeds from a local mill, silk stockings, and nappies, or 'Harrison Squares' as they were called, could be bought.

We had a party on board for some Americans from two 'battle-wagons', the SOUTH DAKOTA and ALABAMA, and some destroyers. A visit to HM Ships was popular with the US Navy as their ships were 'dry'. In fact it was amusing to see their 'gasoline gigs' slipping ashore with the officers and a few cases of liquor to have a party on shore away from their ship. I went aboard our latest battleship, the DUKE OF YORK, to have a look around and was glad I had been appointed to a 'small ship' rather than a big one when I left DORSETSHIRE. I also had a trip on an amphibious Jeep for the first time which was most interesting as another artefact of wartime equipment.

On 9th June we sailed as part of the A/S screen for the joint US/UK battlefleet heading for Jan Mayen and Bear Island in an operation to tempt the TIRPITZ and her consorts to sally forth from their Norwegian ports and give battle. Our force consisted of the SOUTH DAKOTA, ALABAMA, DUKE OF YORK, the aircraft carrier FURIOUS, the cruisers SCYLLA and BERWICK, as well as other supporting US and British destroyers on the screen. The wind was gale force and bitterly cold; we were soon soaking in our recently issued 'Bingham' fur-lined Eskimo type clothing as we plunged along attempting to keep up with the battle-wagons. This you should note was midsummer.

We were also acting as cover for a relief party going to Longyearsby, the coal-mining town in Spitzbergen. Fog rolled in which made station keeping difficult but there was no sign of Jerry except for their Focke-Wulff Kondor flying-boat shadowers which kept well out of range. We turned for home on the 13th, with the Yanks heading back to Iceland, and ourselves to Scapa Flow where we had some 'high-jinks' when OPPORTUNE, complete with their Captain, Cdr Johnny Lee-Barber, boarded us from their whaler at midnight. It was quite a bizarre sight with half the party in pyjamas. They paddled back at 0300.

On the 16th June we were off again down the east coast to Dundee to pick up the aircraft carrier HUNTER and escort her round the north of Scotland to the Clyde. The weather was perfect and we cruised down through the Western Isles which looked marvellous. Arriving at the boom at the entrance to the Firth of Clyde at 0100 on the 17th we frustratingly went about and headed back to Scapa to reach there that afternoon and then to have a boiler-clean. There was no chance of heading south on leave but I gave all-night leave in Kirkwall to some of the crew. The wardroom played hockey with (not against) some very young Wrens and there was a lively evening aboard the destroyer MAHRATTA. After a quick scrub in the floating dry-dock we went out into the Pentland Firth and north to the Orkneys with other ships of the 17th Flotilla on A/S screening exercises and practice shoots, fortunately in good weather.

Back at Scapa I had David Marshall, a Clyde RNVR and a cousin of Kirsteen's, over for dinner from ONSLAUGHT. We chatted about the future of the family firm of shipbuilders, William Simons & Co, of which we were both non-executive directors, and how to put it right – very patronising!

On 2nd July we sailed at 0660 for Skaal Fjord in the Faroes which was a temporary base for a striking force made up of ONSLOW (with Captain (D) aboard) and OBDURATE tasked with patrolling the Iceland/ Faroes Gap with the aim of discouraging the U-boats from breaking into the North Atlantic,

In nice sunny weather we set up inter-ship whaler races and I had some violent exercise pulling in the officers' boat. On the 5th however we were off at noon towards Iceland to follow up a sighting report from a patrolling aircraft; there was now a very welcome Coastal Command presence of Catalinas, Liberators and Flying Fortresses with whom we worked closely. This co-operation with Coastal Command, who now had many more aircraft, made for a much more effective anti-U-boat force, as their coverage for sighting surfaced U-boats, not to mention their depth-charge striking ability, together with our Asdic and attacking power, gradually wore down the enemy. By early autumn 1943 it could be said that we had overcome Dönitz's wolf-pack strategy. Additionally, in between the running of the Russian convoys, usually made up of fifty or sixty merchant ships and requiring all the Fleet destroyers available for close and battleship/cruiser escort duty, there were periods when the destroyers were formed into Escort Groups. These were rushed to back up the frigate and corvette escort groups shepherding the Atlantic convoys to and from the UK being threatened by the U-boat wolf-packs.

So it was in one of these interludes that the 'Os' of the 17th DF were deployed to the Faroes/Iceland gap. The weather was pleasant that July, as well it might be in even a northern summer, and football matches were organised between the ships of the flotilla with the opportunity for plenty of exercise ashore. We even had walk-up shoots stalking guillemots and ptarmigan with Tommy guns in the single shot mode. The capital, Thorshaven, even had shops that stocked 'goodies' such as silk stockings and nappies not now obtainable at home – we posted them back.

Several sorties over the next couple of weeks, following sightings by Coastal Command and in company with ONSLOW, OBDURATE and OPPORTUNE, produced no contacts and eventually on 17th July we returned to Scapa Flow. A day was spent in the Pentland Firth exercising screening tactics with the US battleship SOUTH DAKOTA and the DUKE OF YORK, and then we were off down the Minches with OBEDIENT and ORIBI to rendezvous at the Clyde Light Vessel with the old MALAYA and the 'Woolworth' carrier UNICORN and escort them back to Scapa. It was very frustrating that I did not have even one night alongside so that I could get home to see Kirsteen who was nearing the end of what seemed a very long pregnancy, with erratic help and support at home.

At Scapa we had an official inspection of the ship by Captain (D), Cdr 'Bes' McCoy, and as the standard reflected the First Lieutenant's efforts I was pleased to receive full marks. On 26th July we set off again for the Faroes in company with ORIBI and an oiler. The next day at midnight we sailed to rendezvous with the cruiser BELFAST at 0300 for an operation off the Norwegian coast. We were soon spotted by Blohm & Voss 138 flying-boat shadowers but these were attacked and shot down by our Beaufighter covering escort; we tried to pick up two of the ditched air crew but they were dead and we couldn't fish them out of the water.

Shortly thereafter we met up with the USS ALABAMA, the ILLUSTRIOUS and the ANSON about 100 miles off the Norwegian coast. I'm not sure what was the object of the venture, but perhaps it was another sweep by the Home Fleet to tempt the TIRPITZ and VON SCHEER out of their lairs in the Norwegian fjords. With the sortie over, ORIBI and ourselves returned to the Faroes at 0500 on 29th July to oil, and then sailed again at 2030 to resume the U-boat patrol in company with Captain (D) in MILNE and MAHRATTA, two of the most powerful destroyers in the fleet. They had displacements of nearly 2000 tons, 48,000 HP, power driven turrets with 4.7" guns, and two quadruple torpedo tubes.

In the latitudes we were patrolling there were the most spectacular golden sunsets at around midnight, dropping down over the snow-capped mountains of Iceland. However the weather soon turned raw and cold: a real contrast to the August Bank holiday weather and the happy crowds described in the BBC news. When we returned to Thørshaven I declared a 'make and mend' – a holiday as modest compensation for the days of watchkeeping and discomfort which was backed up by the arrival of the miracle mail. I had been phoning home at every opportunity to monitor the progress of Kirsteen's pregnancy but no news so far, although she was fit and well. Strangely it was easier to get through to the UK from the Faroes than from the Orkneys: obviously traffic was lighter.

The local Bank Holiday ' make and mend' on the 2nd was rudely terminated by orders to follow up a U-boat sighting report and off we went at 2300 at 30 knots with the ship vibrating: my diary notes *"hence the wiggles"*. This time there was some action. A Fortress had dropped a depth charge on a diving U-boat and although we kept 'pinging' with the ASDIC for the target she slipped away. Next morning on 4th August at 0930 we sighted smoke on the horizon and made for it at full speed to find a Sunderland squatting on the sea after depth-charging a U-boat on the surface and herself being shot down. The U-boat was damaged and could not dive and on our arrival at 0958 she set off scuttling charges and the crew took to their life rafts. We picked up 33 of her crew and on calling up the CASTLETON, a Captain Class frigate, she collected the remainder of the U-boat crew, also some of the crew of the Sunderland, taking them on to Iceland. The Coastal Command Sunderland had a Canadian crew of six - the captain being Flying Officer Bishop from Erskine, Alberta. One of his crew had been killed whom we later buried at sea together with a German Engineer officer. It was the first time that I had taken a burial service, one of my duties as First Lieutenant at sea. I used the C of E prayer book; the bodies were sewn into weighted canvas shrouds (made from hammocks) and covered by the Union Jack and the German ensign respectively, then slid over the stern at the appropriate moment. One of the prisoners was the pilot of a Blohm & Voss 138 flying-boat which had been shot down by a Beaufighter the previous Wednesday when he had been shadowing us on our sortie with the Home Fleet off the Norwegian Coast, and had been picked up by the U-boat, U489 – lucky Jerry.

We took the prisoners down to Thurso by 0800 on 5th August and by 1000 were back oiling at Scapa. On the 6th we closed with the DUKE OF YORK in the Fleet anchorage at 0900 and embarked the First Lord of the Admiralty A V Alexander, the Minister of Labour, Malcolm McAlpine and someone important called Methven for a passage to Scrabster. A destroyer belting across the Pentland Firth isn't the most comfortable of conveyances and whilst it was fun for us to meet them, I don't think they enjoyed the trip.

We carried on to Rosyth for a welcome boiler clean and short leave on Saturday 7th August and my father came through in the evening and took me to Arnwood Drive where we all sat around waiting for the arrival of the babe. Of all things Kirsteen had developed chicken-pox and couldn't go into a nursing home for fear of spreading the infection. The gynaecologist, Hector McLellan, found it all most interesting and I remember him asking me to let him know in years to come if the child ever developed chicken-pox as he thought being born with the infection might immunise him for life. Anyway, I went to stay the night with Dad at his flat in Kelvin Court as Arnwood Drive was crowded with Mrs Orr, nurses, etc. I went back the next night (the 9th) to sleep in the lounge chair and Kirsteen woke me at 3 o'clock to alert me that things were happening. I dozed off again but Michael eventually appeared at a quarter past six with our family doctor, Dr Cuthbert, in attendance. All was well but I had to return to ORWELL that morning and left for Rosyth at 0800. When Paddy Satow returned on board later that day I dashed back home and had a couple of days with Kirsteen and Michael. Sue was down at Ayr with the Orrs. Pat Adam, our delightful RNVR doc on ORWELL, who hadn't long graduated from Edinburgh University and recently been married, came through from Rosyth and paid us a much appreciated visit.

Glasgow Herald, 10th August 1943
Son Michael's Birth Announcement

> **MILLER.** – At 9 Arnwood Drive, Glasgow, W.2. on 9th August 1943, to Kirsteen, wife of Lieutenant Alan J. M. Miller, D.S.C., R.N.V.R., a son.

I was back on board early on the 13th and off once again to Scapa although I was feeling lousy with a touch of flu and a temperature of 101°. The good news was that the promotion of our Sub-Lieutenant, Ian Scrimgeour-Wedderburn (known as Scrym), to Lieutenant had come through. This called for a party but I was only fit to crawl out of my bunk whenever I felt strong enough. King George VI was in Scapa on board the DUKE OF YORK so off we went exercising in the Pentland Firth to show off our latest battleship. When we returned in the evening covered in salt spray from the high speed manoeuvres I was feeling worse than ever and Doc sent for a specialist from the Scapa-based hospital ship, ISLE OF JERSEY, who diagnosed glandular fever. So on the 15th August I was sent over to her whilst ORWELL went off on an estimated two week operation. Paddy Satow temporarily took over as No 1.

There had been an amusing incident two days previously: as soon as we shackled to the buoy in Gutter Sound on return from the manoeuvres with the DUKE OF YORK, a signal came from the Fleet anchorage *"His Majesty requests the pleasure of the company (RPC)*[34] *of Sub-Lieutenant I A S Wedderburn to dinner, etc, etc. Barge will collect at 2100hrs"*. This threw us all into a panic as first it meant that a salt-encrusted Scrym had to have a bath ahead of the Captain, upsetting the normal hierarchy for this ritual (we only had one bath for the officers). After this we scratched around for the best items of uniform, a clean shirt and a shower of 'fou-fou'[35] so that he would smell nice. Hard-up Sub-Lieutenants weren't noted for smart uniforms but wearing Satow's jacket with the two stripes he went off in the Admiral's barge looking and smelling well to dine with The King. Apparently Scrym's father had been a shipmate or equerry of George VI at some time or other which was the reason for the summons. Although The King knew of Scrym's promotion to Lieutenant, his Flag Lieutenant did not. Meanwhile the Captain entertained on board his brother-in-law, Cdr Woodruffe RN, he of the hilarious broadcast from the BBC at the 1938 Spithead Review when he had had a few too many and kept declaring *"The Fleet's all lit up"*.

I quickly recovered from whatever it was and was sent off on 7 days' leave which was never unwelcome. I bounced a passage south from Hatston Airfield at Kirkwall on the shuttle flight to Donibristle in Fife. The aircraft was a De Haviland Rapide, a biplane with pointed wings used to transport men and freight on this route. The take-off from Hatston was memorable; on the journey north the plane must have been carrying freight as the seats had been unbolted and stowed to be relocated for the flight south. Unfortunately although replaced and available for us to take our places ready for take-off some 'erk' had

---

[34] 'RPC' is the standard naval signal for "Request the pleasure of your company", the reply being 'WMP' – "With much pleasure" or 'MRU' – "Much regret unable".
[35] Talcum powder.

omitted to bolt them down and as we rushed along the runway with seatbelts on, seats and passengers ended up in a tangled heap at the back of the cabin. The pilot was pretty smart to adjust for this rapid change in the trim of the plane and all was well.

A week later I received a wire to stay on leave until further notice; intriguing but welcome. This was then countermanded by a further wire from the Principal Medical Officer (PMO) on the ISLE OF JERSEY to say I had to return there for a further check-up. This meant a run through to Donibristle and a flight up to the Orkneys for five minutes with the PMO. However, after dinner with my old friend Acworth of DORSETSHIRE days, now in command of the 'R' Class destroyer ROCKET, I returned south the next day, again by plane, this time having checked the seat fastenings were secure.

ORWELL's operation, which I was sorry to have missed, was to escort the battleship RENOWN taking Churchill to the Quebec Conference and back again. It was an uneventful passage both ways by all accounts with a pleasant spell in St John's, Newfoundland while the leaders conferred. As my cabin was empty on ORWELL, it accommodated the writer and rhymer A P Herbert for the trip, who presumably was a speech-writer in the Prime Minister's party. He exchanged impromptu verses with Mary Churchill in RENOWN on the Aldis.

I was left on unscheduled leave until the middle of September when ORWELL was due back but this time I had to make my way to Thurso by train and the steamer over to Scapa. Back on board Pat Adam had not forgotten me and had bought me lots of 'goodies', in particular gallon tins of maple syrup which was a rare treat for the sugar starved family when eventually I managed to take it home.

On 21st September it was *"raise steam with all despatch"* and off to Londonderry in company with ORIBI, MUSKETEER and ORKAN. ORKAN, although an 'O' was in fact one of the larger and more powerful 'M' Class, manned by Poles from commissioning day. The intelligence was that there was a second U-boat offensive being mounted by Dönitz after he had withdrawn his U-boats following the set-back to his wolf-pack offensive in May. We put in hours of intensive anti-submarine tactical training as a Group off Larne returning to Londonderry on occasions. Paddy Satow's 'draft chit' came through and his relief, Sub Lt Pelly, arrived. Despite his intellectual brilliance I wasn't sorry to see Satow move on as he was a hopeless organiser and had turned ORWELL's ship company into a disgruntled state whilst I had been away. His career in the Navy came to a discreditable conclusion.

ONS 19 to Newfoundland

With news of a U-boat picket line forming well to the north we were despatched on 28th September as the 3rd Escort Group to support the close escort of the slow west-bound convoy ONS[36] 19 being diverted towards Greenland in an attempt to skirt round the enemy. The weather was stormy and of course cold as we took our stations on the outer perimeter of the convoy with our 'Huff-Duff' on a constant sweep of the horizon to catch any U-boat transmissions. The ASDIC also 'pinged' away to locate the underwater foe. The ASDIC operator lived in a cubicle on the bridge, rather like a small telephone box, constantly turning a wheel with a pointer round a 360° card which indicated the direction of the beam transmitted every few seconds from the ASDIC dome located under the hull. This transmission was accompanied by a distinctive 'ping' which faded away if it was not interrupted by an underwater object such as a submarine. If there was a contact it produced a Doppler effect echo which indicated the range on the operator's headphones and through a loudspeaker on the bridge. The ASDIC equipment was constantly manned and switched on as soon as we left harbour so this 'ping' became a sub-conscious background noise which only the operator's *"echo bearing ...... degrees"* alerted the Officer of the Watch.

---

[36] 'ONS' – Outward-bound convoys from the UK; 'HNS' – Homeward-bound.

The U-boat pack was definitely near but so far the ordered diversions of the convoy had enabled us to avoid them. ORWELL had to break off the screen to oil so we headed for Hvalfjord in Iceland on 2nd October and rejoined on the 3rd right up in 60°N at 28°W near the tip of Greenland. It was exceptionally stormy and cold, and the convoy was making slow progress. There were U-boats all around but the diversions ordered by Western Approaches Headquarters were so far effective although the following convoy was not so fortunate and was being attacked. It was again prudent to oil but this we did for the first time by a buoyant hose trailed from the stern of an oiler in the convoy which was hazardous but successful and not too messy an operation. Looking down from the bridge I felt sorry for Pelly and the foc'sle party wrestling with the hose in the rough seas and being drenched by the chilling spray.

So far, so good, having dodged the U-boats and allowing the slow convoy to proceed unharmed on its way westwards while our 3rd Escort Group was ordered to join the escort of a large homeward-bound convoy threatened by the same wolf-pack. Towards dusk in a high wind and sea our 'Huff-Duff' sets in the four destroyers gave us a fix on a group of U-boats about 12 miles off signalling to each other and their headquarters in Lorient. We ran down the bearing and kept an estimated five U-boats from surfacing all night while the convoy passed safely by. However we didn't escape unscathed. At about 0400 just when I was about to go on watch and having an overall 'cat's lick' of a wash in my cabin I heard a high pitched whine passing under the ship, followed about 3 minutes later by the deep thud of an explosion; this was a torpedo which miraculously passed under us and sank the Polish manned ORKAN in station on our beam[1]. I would have been embarrassed appearing at the pearly gates with no clothes on.

---

[1] Post-war records divulge that it was U610, commanded by Kapitän-Leutnant Baron Walther von Freyburg-Eisenburg-Allmedingen, which fired the torpedo, but quick retribution came later in the battle when U610 was sunk with all hands by Sunderland 'J' of 422 Squadron, RCAF. The Baron has beaten me to the 'Pearly Gates'.

MUSKETEER picked up 43 survivors while ORIBI and ourselves continued to seek out the enemy. In the morning when air cover arrived four U-boats were sunk by Coastal Command Fortresses and we took aboard 18 survivors including the Captain, Hans Spiedal and his terrier, Adelbert, which John Hodges adopted. The convoy only lost one ship, from which there were several survivors, so apart from the tragedy of ORKAN we reckoned it had been a successful battle.

In a much quieter sea we steamed along with ORIBI to the Clyde and being a Sunday I took Church on the for'd messdeck, not a very common practise at sea in destroyers, but I had a feeling the crew would welcome a formal opportunity to gather and pray together after what we had been through. Once again I had to conduct a burial service of two Germans who had died from their wounds. After setting the scene on the quarterdeck, with our ensign at half-mast, and their mess-mates brought up from below, together with Oberleutnant Spiedal, their Captain, I was beginning to read the burial service when Spiedal interrupted me. He launched into a long tirade about Hitler and the Fatherland which, knowing a bit of German I, in part, understood. It finished up with *"Heil Hitler"*. I had a feeling the poor victims' messmates would have better appreciated a proper Christian burial service. As an officer POW he messed in the wardroom and had a cabin allocated, but he was a surly character and rude to the wardroom stewards who got their own back by serving him bad boiled eggs and indulged in noisy laughter when he stormed off to his cabin.

We arrived in the Clyde at 0200 on 10th October in pouring rain and early in the morning handed the prisoners over to the Army. I had phoned Kirsteen by then and she arrived down at 11 o'clock with brother Kenneth, who had just returned from Italy where he was Gunnery officer on the cruiser EURAYALUS. We didn't have much time alone as we were due to sail for Scapa at 1430. I landed all my tins of maple syrup and other 'goodies' from Newfoundland so all in all it was a worthwhile and opportune diversion. It was a wild party night after we shackled to the buoy at Gutter Sound in Scapa and not realising that even destroyers seemed to have swing doors, Doc Adam with an unsteady hand, had to fix me up with two stitches in my forehead. We had a couple of days relaxation with walks ashore whilst we were in dry dock for a bottom scrub and a coat of paint in the latest variegated pastel shades of camouflage.

Spitzbergen and JWS54(A) to Murmansk

After leaving dock on 14th October we sailed with ONSLAUGHT, ORIBI and the USS FITCH to Seidisfjord in the east of Iceland to join up with the heavy cruiser TUSCALOOSA for an operation to Spitzbergen. We went alongside TUSCALOOSA and took aboard several tons of stores and a Norwegian captain for the passage. As these stores carried on deck consisted of sulphuric acid and paraffin, I was hoping it was going to be an action free trip. The passage to Spitzbergen[37] was trouble free although it became noticeably colder by the hour with sea and air temperature creeping below zero. Intelligence reported the presence of a U-boat in the fjord. This was later uprated to three and at 1800 on 19th October ONSLAUGHT, in the dark at this time of year, located one on her ASDIC and rammed her near Barentsburg. We set about searching the area but found no trace of the damaged U-boat or any other. We broke off the search as we had to land the stores, so still ASDIC sweeping at high speed, we went into Advent Fjord and alongside at Longyearsby, unloading the stores at 1800. Together with ONSLAUGHT, who had broken her propeller in the collision, we made our way back to Iceland and that night had a fantastic display of the Aurora Borealis or Northern Lights as we passed Jan Mayen Island. Amazing swathes of pale green and yellow, like gauze, floated across the sky to the south for two or three hours. The visibility and clarity of the night were extraordinary. A signal was received that the U-boats had closed Longyearsby and were again shelling the settlement.

---

[37] Svalbard in Norwegian.

After a few days in Scapa good news arrived that we were to have a boiler clean alongside in Greenock. This was the first time in the war that I'd had a break in my 'home port'. With the willing co-operation of my messmates I arranged plenty of leave at home and on Sunday 31st October we christened Michael in Westbourne Church throughout which he yelled the whole time. Two days later we sailed for Scapa at 0900 and spent the rest of the week on intensive exercises in the Pentland Firth during which, on a dark and stormy night, we lost Able Seaman Wood, a fine young man, washed over the side. Despite a long search we saw no sign of him and he wouldn't have survived for long in the cold water of the Firth.

These exercises seemed to go on for ever, even through Sunday; they were very dull and uncomfortable with much of the time spent screening the DUKE OF YORK and HOWE at high speed. I was gradually developing a bout of flu which didn't help my spirits. Added to this the USS FITCH hit us in the dark in Gutter Sound which put us alongside the depot ship TYNE for four days for repairs. Amidst all this it is difficult to maintain the morale amongst the ship's company; even the officers started to squabble and I spent one night drinking and arguing with John Hodges until 0400 over why we disagreed! There is no doubt the Nelsonian adage that *"ships and men rot in harbour"* has truth in it.

All this was to change as we sailed at 1800 on 15th November with the 17th DF with Capt 'Bes' McCoy as Captain (D) in ONSLOW, along with three Canadian destroyers, HURON, IROQUOIS and HAIDA, for Seidisfjord in Iceland as part of an escort for convoy JW54(A) bound for Murmansk. The convoy of 20 merchant ships came in sight off Iceland at 1100 on 18th November and we took station, together with the other destroyers around it, proceeding north-eastwards at $9^{1}/_{2}$ knots in quite good weather.

OBEDIENT dropped out with steering gear trouble and returned to Scapa. The days were getting shorter with dawn at 1030 and it was dark by 1500. We had the luxury of a permanent Coastal Command Catalina sweeping round the convoy in daylight hours and so far we hadn't been sighted by the enemy. By 1700 on the 21st we were 35 miles off Bear Island and 73° N; I noted in my diary that day that I had the luxury of an orange and a bath! The convoy was keeping up its pace of 9$^{1}/_{2}$ knots with no stragglers. On the 23rd we turned southwards towards the Kola Inlet where some of the convoy ships split off and made for Archangel in the White Sea escorted by four Soviet destroyers. We had not been bothered by the enemy and every ship was safely delivered. This happy circumstance had been assisted by the mist and cloud which persisted for most of the time while we were in the real danger zone off the North Cape of Norway. Distant cover was provided by the battleship ANSON, the USS TUSCALOOSA, the cruisers BERMUDA, KENT, and JAMAICA, and four US destroyers. It was well understood in naval circles, even amongst the merchant seamen of the convoys, that the convoy was also a bait to draw out the SCHARNHORST or even the TIRPITZ from their lairs on the Norwegian coast. If they could be brought successfully into battle it would remove the ever-present threat of a 'fleet-in-being' and release our battleships and cruisers for better use elsewhere. As usual we never saw this supporting fleet until we all pitched up in Vaenga near Murmansk.

After milling about all night awaiting our turn to oil, we lay alongside BERMUDA for our stay. BERMUDA's wardroom were extremely hospitable and a rather 'heavy' night ensued. The next day, the 26th, Doc Adam and I went ashore early for some exercise. We borrowed skis from the British hospital where Pat knew the Principal Medical Officer named McEwan from Rutherglen near Glasgow, and clad in our fur-lined Eskimo parkas we set off in the snow towards the wretched town of Murmansk. We had our exercise but the prison-like blocks of apartments and unsmiling inhabitants, who seemed frightened even to acknowledge a greeting, were a lasting impression. We returned to the hospital for lunch and then in the evening there was a splendid concert by a Russian choir aboard BERMUDA for both ships' companies.

The 17th DF set off for home on the 27th November in charge of a small convoy and with the weather remarkably mild and calm we made good speed. It was very dark even during the so-called daylight hours and we had not seen the sun for at least two weeks. By 1st December we received a signal to say we had been sighted so trouble was imminent; at 0500 the destroyer INCONSTANT at the rear of the convoy spotted a U-boat on the surface and attacked, resulting in an estimated kill. Ourselves and ONSLAUGHT swept back and searched for a couple of hours but no contact was made so we rejoined the convoy screen. Throughout the next couple of days U-boats made sighting reports of the convoy but no attacks developed. We also heard that six Focke-Wulffs took off from Trondheim at 1130 but fortunately they never found us.

Turning south-west on passing Bear Island the length of daylight improved but still no sun appeared. It turned very cold; the guard-rails iced up and there was a dangerous amount of ice on the deck. We left the convoy at 1800 on 5th December with Iceland in sight below a lovely sunset of pale blue and gold and put into Seidisfjord on the east coast to oil. It was blowing a gale there and we had an appalling night trying to secure to the oiler despite bright moonlight on the snow covered mountains illuminating the whole weird scene. Exhausted, I stayed in my bunk the next day until 1130 as we made our way back to Scapa!

The Strategic Scene

A word now about the strategic background to all this activity, and an explanation of the intense exercising with the 'battle-wagons' and cruisers of the Home Fleet. Convoys to Russia had been suspended in May as it was considered to be too hazardous to send them through in the long daylight hours of the summer months when they were exposed to the Luftwaffe based in nearby northern Norway. Churchill and Stalin were also engaged in acrimonious discussions about the reception and facilities provided for our merchant seamen who often had to spend weeks in Murmansk and Archangel whilst their ships were slowly unloaded. Anthony Eden was sent to Moscow at this time to try to resolve the impasse.

There was also a change in the Naval command structure: Dudley Pound, the First Sea Lord, who had returned from meetings in Washington in the RENOWN with Churchill in August, escorted by ORWELL as recounted earlier, fell ill shortly after and died in October. He had been an excellent and highly respected First Sea Lord and had literally worked himself to death. His place was taken by Admiral Sir Andrew Cunningham. At the same time, Admiral Jack Tovey, for whom I had great regard but who had fallen out with Churchill, was replaced by Admiral Bruce Fraser as CinC Home Fleet. Incidentally Kirsteen's lifelong friend, Catriona Anderson, was for several years a 1st Officer Wren on Bruce Fraser's staff, even accompanying him to Japan towards the end of the war. When travelling with him around Scotland, Catriona was most enterprising at visiting farmhouses and coming to Arnwood Drive with eggs and chickens for Kirsteen and the children.

While presumably the prime objective of the Russian convoys was to deliver tanks, aircraft and other war supplies to our Ally, Bruce Fraser was equally determined to bring the German 'fleet-in-being', lurking in Altenfjord on the coast of Norway, into battle. This force consisting of the TIRPITZ, SCHARNHORST and attendant powerful 'Z' Class destroyers made a rather strange and somewhat pathetic sortie for such a powerful fleet to raid Spitzbergen on 8th September. They destroyed Longyearsby and Barentsburg with their 15" and 11" guns. The Norwegian residents managed to send out a signal and the Home Fleet left Scapa in response but the German ships quickly beat a retreat to the safety of Altenfjord. It was five weeks later that we went to Spitzbergen with the USS TUSCALOOSA to re-establish the base at Barentsburg and Longyearsby with stores and Free Norwegian troops.

It was clear to Bruce Fraser that the Kriegsmarine was alive and well and he must have been a bit irked that the bait of the first convoy, JW54(A), of the new fishing season was not taken. It was also at this time that the energetic Dönitz had replaced Raeder as the Grossadmiral of the Kriegsmarine and still had Hitler's confidence, although Hitler was never very supportive of the German Navy's actions. Since the defeat of the U-boat wolf-pack offensive in the early part of the summer from May – July in 1943, two new weapons were coming into the U-boat service which boosted their capability. The first was the development of the 'snorkel', a tube protruding above the waves from the conning tower through which the air intake and exhaust ran for the diesel motors. This enabled the boats to run just beneath the surface on their main engines thereby extending their underwater range immeasurably. The second was the T-5 acoustic torpedo called by us the 'Gnat' which homed in on the noise of a ship's propellers and exploded in close proximity to the vessel neatly blowing off her stern. With these gadgets the U-boats' targets seemed to shift from the merchantmen to the escorts. Both the 'Gnat' homing torpedo and the snorkel proved to be effective additions to the U-boats' armament and if they had been introduced earlier in the conflict they would certainly have affected our increasing and timely ascendancy over the wolf-packs. At that time there were no effective counter-measures to the 'Gnat' apart from intense and tiring concentration by the ASDIC operators to detect an approaching acoustic torpedo and instant action by the OOW on the bridge to release a depth charge and instantly increase speed. We had to be on the alert for them every minute of the night and day. Later the Americans developed a device called 'Foxer', a clapper trailed over the stern which set off the 'Gnat' before it reached you.

A few days' rest in Scapa in early December gave us the opportunity for a 'run-ashore' and patiently to hang around a telephone hoping to get a call through to home. However we weren't left alone for long and on the 10th we started more exercises off the Shetlands with the Home Fleet cruiser squadrons practising fleet manoeuvres and dummy torpedo attacks on the 'enemy' cruiser. Fortunately for this time of year the weather was fine and we did not become too wet and cold.

When we returned to Scapa the Captain was in his bunk with 'flu and for the first time I had to take ORWELL alongside the oiler and then to anchor in the Flow. This was followed by a boiler clean beside the depot ship TYNE which precluded us from crashing about on exercises for the time being. I took the opportunity for long walks ashore with 'Adelbert', the terrier John Hodges had 'half-inched' from

Oberleutnant Spiedal, the U-boat captain whom we had rescued from U-489. I recall I had taken 'Adelbert' home with me to Arnwood Drive during our previous boiler-clean at Greenock in October when John Hodges had gone south on leave. This nice enemy dog may have been submarine trained but wasn't house trained nor did we bother about the quarantine regulations! John kept him for some years after the war.

News was filtering through of the successful attack on the battleship TIRPITZ at Altenfjord by six midget submarines which put her out of action for many months and removed this major threat to the resumed programme of Arctic convoys. Of the six midget submarines known as X-craft, two penetrated the defence network round the TIRPITZ in Altenfjord and placed their charges beneath the battleship where they duly exploded. Lt Cameron of X6 and Lt Place of X7 were captured but awarded Victoria Crosses which they received after their release at the end of the war. Ten other officers and men were lost from the other X-craft that were detected and sunk. As the pocket battleship LUTZOW had left Altenfjord the day after this attack and reached the Baltic safely, despite attempts by the RAF and Fleet Air Arm to intercept her, this left only the SCHARNHORST and five Z-class destroyers in the Northern Task Force.

Chapter XIII

CONVOY JW55A AND
THE SINKING OF THE SCHARNHORST
20th December 1943 – 8th January 1944

Our incessant exercising with the capital ships of the Home Fleet, such as the DUKE OF YORK with Admiral Sir Bruce Fraser aboard, and the cruiser squadrons led by Vice Admiral Robert Burnett in BELFAST, convinced us that Fraser was seriously expecting an attack by surface ships on an early convoy to Russia. The U-boats of course were routinely deployed on a line from Bear Island to the Norwegian coast, closing in as a pack once the convoy had been sighted by one of their number or a reconnaissance Focke-Wulff.

December was a month of wild storms around the Orkneys and even in Scapa Flow we dragged with two anchors on eight shackles[38] of chain cable. The barometer was down to 956mb. On the 20th it eased and we returned to a buoy to load up with mail and some service passengers for Russia. With a call into the Faroes to top up with oil we sailed at midnight on the 21st to join convoy JW55A which consisted of 18 ships doing 10 knots. The main ocean escort consisted of ten Fleet destroyers[39] with our Captain (D), Bes McCoy, in ONSLOW as Senior Officer, plus two corvettes, OXLIP and HONEYSUCKLE, and the minesweeper GLEANER as rescue ship.

Although we as foot soldiers in the escorts were not party to the intelligence signals that were emanating from the Admiralty, I learnt after the war that Ultra had revealed intense aerial reconnaissance and an order on 18th December to the SCHARNHORST group under the command of Admiral Bey to come to three hours notice for sea.

---

[38] 10 fathom lengths of chain cable.

[39] ONSLAUGHT, ORWELL, IMPULSIVE, OBDURATE, IROQUOIS, HURON, HAIDA, WHITEHALL, and WRESTLER

This confirmed to Fraser that there would be a surface attack on our convoy which would give him the opportunity to bring the SCHARNHORST into battle.

A convoy of nineteen empty ships in convoy, RA55B, was leaving Murmansk for home on 23rd December escorted by cruisers and ten destroyers; this convoy was first detected by German air-reconnaissance and shadowed until Christmas Eve but eventually reached Iceland safely. When Fraser had decided RA55A was sufficiently to the west to be out of danger he broke wireless silence, a most unusual move, and instructed CS10, Admiral Burnett in BELFAST, at 0200 on 25th December to detach four destroyers, MUSKETEER, MATCHLESS, OPPORTUNE and VIRAGO from RA55A to join JW55A. This brought our Fleet destroyer strength up to fourteen which gave the convoy escort considerable clout in itself.

We had been sighted by a Heinkel 177 'snooper' on the 22nd which was engaged by IROQUOIS (a Canadian Tribal Class destroyer) for about an hour, and again on the 23rd JU88s attacked us intermittently for about 10 hours and were homing the U-boats onto us. With our strong escort we kept at least two down with depth charges and they did no harm.

By this time we were approaching Bear Island with the weather deteriorating with heavy cloud and a rising sea to add to the discomfort of more or less perpetual darkness, and at this latitude of 74°N, close to the edge of the Arctic ice, the decks, guns and superstructure were becoming encrusted with ice. At 0319, early on the morning of the 26th Dec, Boxing Day, the Admiralty signalled to all ships involved in the operation that the *"Admiralty appreciated that the SCHARNHORST was at sea"*; it could be assumed her screen of heavily armed 'Z' Class destroyers would be in company. This was followed by a signal from Admiral Fraser to Capt McCoy at 0705 to alter the course of the convoy to the north-east which proved to be a difficult and lengthy manoeuvre as the gale which had caused several of the merchantmen to fall behind was now veering to the south; this also indicated another depression was on its way but probably meant a welcome rise in temperature and rain instead of snow.

In the developing situation it was imperative that the convoy should keep together so we slowed down to allow the stragglers to close up. Shortly after noon the four destroyers, MUSKETEER, MATCHLESS, OPPORTUNE and VIRAGO, joined our screen and came under McCoy's control. At about this point Admiral Bruce Fraser began to take tactical charge and relaxed the Navy's strict discipline of wireless silence unless in direct contact with the enemy. Normally the Admiralty could speak to you but no ship ever used its radio to communicate with shore or another ship. One of the surprising weaknesses of the U-boats which we exploited with our shipboard HF/DF was their daily routine reporting of their positions on patrol to their bases.

Anyway, Fraser now established a plain language link on the inter-ship radio-telephone, known as the 'TBS'[40], with CS10, Bob Burnett in BELFAST. We and all the other ships could listen to their exchanges. They didn't chatter but kept up a stream of brief signals encompassing the ever-changing drama of the battle. I did two things with this unique opportunity: I kept a copy of all the signals written down by our ORWELL telegraphists, and patched the linked transmissions on the TBS used by Fraser and Burnett over the Tannoy system in ORWELL. This allowed the crew whether on watch or down below to hear the commentary on the battle as it developed.

On Christmas Day we were now past Bear Island but still heading 045° to the north-east with the weather blowing at Force 7 with rain and visibility down to about 2 miles. U-boats were now our immediate concern as we intercepted on HF/DF their sighting signals of the convoy to base. We did a very wet sweep in their direction in the afternoon but they (there were at least two) probably spotted the formidable size of the escort (not only the 14 destroyers but the two corvettes as well) and kept their heads down.

---

[40] TBS: Talk between Ships

At 0600 on Boxing Day Captain (D) received a signal from the CinC to alter the course of the convoy further to the north and we settled on 035°; the same time CS10 and his cruisers BELFAST, NORFOLK and SHEFFIELD started closing on us from the east. The CinC in DUKE OF YORK had the cruiser JAMAICA and four Fleet destroyers, near-sister ships of ORWELL, the SAUMAREZ, SAVAGE, SCORPION, and the Norwegian manned STORD with him and his ships, known as Force 2, were coming into the fray from the west.

I had stood down from my normal night watch of 0400-0800 (actually they were all 'night' watches in these latitudes), had some breakfast, a wash and shave, and returned to the bridge. Suddenly from BELFAST at 0846 came a signal *"Jig 295 – 16"* which translated means "radar echo bearing 295° 16 miles". This triggered the first phase of the oncoming battle. At 0927 it was followed by *"Nuts 190 – 7"* meaning "Enemy bearing 190° at 7 miles" and then the flash of gunfire far on our starboard bow. CS10's cruisers had opened fire at an unidentified ship heading on a northerly course, which subsequently altered to a southerly one. Then at 0921 the SCHARNHORST was sighted by SHEFFIELD at 6 miles. All three cruisers fired starshell to illuminate the target and these were the flashes we saw from our bridge. Burnett then ordered his cruisers to open serious fire but in altering course to close the range BELFAST and SHEFFIELD blanketed their own 'X' after-turrets. NORFOLK however had all guns bearing and at 0930 fired six broadsides with her 8" guns at 9800 yards and scored three hits on the battle-cruiser destroying her port high-angle director and radar aerial; the latter a vital fitting in the seamless darkness of day and night.

SCHARNHORST made off to the south-east at speed, by no means giving up, then worked her way round to the north to attack our convoy. Meanwhile the convoy had been ordered onto a northerly course to keep clear of the battle-zone. At the same time the four destroyers that had joined the convoy screen on Christmas day were ordered to rejoin CS10's cruisers which had closed our convoy: their primary task was the safe passage of the merchant ships. The cruisers now with

MUSKETEER, MATCHLESS, OPPORTUNE and VIRAGO took a position some 10 miles ahead, with us on their port quarter. The convoy was now getting too close to the edge of the ice so McCoy had to alter our course to 125° just south of east.

Due to the certain presence of U-boats the cruisers zigzagged at 28 knots behind their screen of four destroyers but the state of the sea soon forced Burnett to reduce to 18 knots as the destroyers were unable to maintain station. Meanwhile we ploughed on at about 8 knots with the convoy on a course of 125°. At 1213 came a signal from SHEFFIELD *"Radar echo bearing 070-12 miles"* followed by BELFAST at 1222 signalling *"Enemy in sight"* at 8 miles; all three cruisers opened broadside fire at 10,000 yards. CS10's destroyers were ordered to attack SCHARNHORST with torpedoes but in fact they never managed to gain bearing into an attacking position. Poor NORFOLK, which was the only cruiser not supplied with flashless cordite shells for her 8" guns, became SCHARNHORST's target and received two hits from her 11" guns: this caused considerable damage putting 'X' turret and her radars out of action together with killing seven men and leaving five wounded.

SCHARNHORST was hit but not slowed down, making off at high speed out of sight to the south-east towards her Norwegian base. She was not out of radar range however and Burnett with his cruisers settled down to a stern pursuit at 28 knots. As long as SCHARNHORST continued on her present course she was of no danger to the convoy. Meanwhile what of Admiral Bey's five 'Z' Class destroyers? They were not in company with SCHARNHORST as one would have expected and could have fallen on us at any time. So, Captain (D) formed the Fleet destroyers of the escort into the classic and much exercised torpedo attacking formation, and positioned the two divisions along the flanks of the convoy between it and the expected approach course of the German destroyers. This was what all the thrashing about the Pentland Firth had been in anticipation.

The answer to the disappearance of the German destroyers was only explained from records available after the war. At about noon

Admiral Bey had ordered his destroyers, under command of Capt Johanneson, who had had difficulty in keeping up with the SCHARNHORST in the rough gale force conditions, to detach and make a sweep independently to the south-west in the hope of finding the convoy. In doing so they passed within eight miles of us. Surprisingly neither the radar equipment of our destroyers (which was of the latest type) nor the enemy's detected each other. Perhaps the wild weather had a hand in this. The 'Z' Class destroyers were in any case not very suitable for operating in the heavy weather and seas experienced in the Barents Sea as their 5·5" guns and eight torpedo tubes made them top heavy causing them to roll excessively. Compounding their problems was the lack of sea time and practice put in by their crews due to the need to conserve fuel oil compared with the time spent at sea by the British flotillas. Anyway they completely lost touch with the SCHARNHORST now speeding south-east towards Norway and never saw her again. At about noon Admiral Bey received a signal from Capt Johanneson reporting that he hadn't found the convoy so Bey unaccountably sent them back to Altenfjord at a time when he must have perceived a real need for support from his destroyers.

The SCHARNHORST was still heading at full speed south-east towards Norway, being shadowed by BELFAST's radar from over the horizon, while DUKE OF YORK with JAMAICA and her destroyers were approaching flat out at 29 knots from the south-west in the hope of cutting SCHARNHORST off before she reached her refuge. Suddenly at 1606 a clear blip at 22 miles appeared on BELFAST's radar screen indicating the enemy still steering 150° and therefore trapped in a pincer between the British Forces 1 and 2. When Fraser had closed to six miles (remember all in an over-clouded black and stormy night), he opened fire with a full broadside of 14" guns after illuminating the enemy with starshell from his 5·25" secondary armament. The SCHARNHORST was apparently taken by surprise as at that moment her guns were seen to be still trained fore and aft. On her quarter astern, JAMAICA opened fire with her 6" guns. At this range and with radar fire control, hits were immediately registered and

SCHARNHORST swung away to the north heading towards Burnett's cruisers of Force 1. These ships also opened fire forcing the enemy to alter course again to the east in the hope of escaping. She could still maintain her superior speed and there was a chance she would pull away. It was now just after 1700 and a long and potentially losing race ensued although DUKE OF YORK continued to fire at the enemy until the range had opened to 20,000 yards. In the meantime Fraser had ordered his four faithful destroyers, SAUMAREZ and SAVAGE to port, STORD (Norwegian manned) and SCORPION to starboard, all of whom had an incredibly tough time maintaining station at high speed in these conditions, to prepare for a torpedo attack. They had been desperately trying to 'gain bearing' on the German to reach a position from which they could fire their torpedoes. At 1820 fortune (or rather the DUKE OF YORK's guns) suddenly favoured them when SCHARNHORST's speed, after a hit in the engine room, fell to 22 knots and her guns ceased firing. This enabled the destroyers to creep up on the port and starboard quarters where they were not spotted by the Germans until they were two miles away. They then started to fire starshell over the great ship who immediately opened up her secondary and anti-aircraft armament at the destroyers and altered course to starboard to comb their anticipated torpedo tracks. This in fact threw her into the torpedoes of STORD, and SCORPION fired on her starboard side: one of eight found their target. Again this alteration of course by the enemy gave SAVAGE and SAUMAREZ their chance and two torpedoes were sent into SCHARNHORST at almost point blank range, reducing her speed to 10 knots.

This enabled our big ships to move in for the kill with their guns and yet more torpedoes until at 2130 the CinC sent a message to the Admiralty *"SCHARNHORST sunk"*. She took 1765 officers and men with her; SCORPION managed to save thirty, MATCHLESS six. Lt Ian Cox RNVR was the officer in charge of the radar screens on DUKE OF YORK and reported to Admiral Bruce Fraser that the SCHARNHORST's echo was finally fading as she rolled over and sank. No-one on any of the British ships actually saw her go. This, the last

RECORD OF SIGNALS INTERCEPTED ON HMS ORWELL DURING THE BATTLE AND SINKING OF THE GERMAN BATTLE-CRUISER 'SCHARNHORST' ON CHRISTMAS AND BOXING DAY 1943

PAGE 1

XMAS DAY SCHARN AT SEA – 4 dest joined		BELFAST
Belfast		NORFOLK
0846 -	Jig 295 16	SHEFFIELD
0927 -	NUTS 190 7	‖ MUSKETEER
0943 -	D17 Do you require destroyers	‖ MATCHLESS
	YES – MUSKETEER SENT	OPPORTUNE
1000 -	S damaged and made off 040˙	VIRAGO
1004 -	CS10 - 325˙24 kts	
	Closing convoy & keep to North	DUKE OF YORK
	Emergency turns etc.	SAVAGE
1213 -	Sheffield J 070 12	SAUMAREZ
		SCORPIO
1222 -	NUTS - 087 - 8	STORD
	When we saw firing on port bow	JAMAICA
	we formed and patrolled between	
	convoy & battle	
1230 -	NORFOLK HIT - X Turret	
1318 -	S made off 165˙ 28 kts	
	Belfast & Sheffield shadowing – chase started	
	NORFOLK dropped out 1550 - ??? of fire	
1606 -	S - C˙ 150˙	
1612 -	Destroyers told to keep to westward	
1625 -	Sheffield down to 23 kts	
1630 -	Belfast CS 10 by herself – stern chase	
	Enemy bg 212 4.5 miles	
1640 -	Norfolk – I hope to remain with you	
1642 -	CinC NUTS - 020 - 6 miles	
	S – altered 040 - 28	
1700 -	D of Y C˙North	
1720 -	S - OSTA 055˙	
	C in C lost touch asked CS 10 for news	
	Who had Radar contact at 7.5 miles	
1728 -	C in C to destroyers – attack with torpedoes	

KEY	
'NUTS'	- Enemy
'JIG' or 'J'	- Radar bearing contact
'CS 10'	- Burnett in BELFAST
'S'	- SCHARNHORST

PAGE 2

> *C in C doing 27 but could not catch*

Destroyers signalled am endeavouring
to obtain bearing   1730 - 1850   1-20 mins

1814   *Scorpion asked to report fall of shot*

1840 - *Scorpion gave Nuts*

1849 - *C in C to CS 10.   I see little hope of catching*
         Dramatic decision   S and am proceeding to support
         > *Convoy*

1850 - *Savage   - train tubes port*
         Probably 4 knot advantage at most.

1856 - *attack completed*

1858 - *C in C anxious asks for report*

1905 - *Scorpion reports possible hit portside*

1912 - *Savage estimates enemy speed   20 kts*

1918 - *Enemy turns west*

1927 - *Jamaica ordered to attack with torpedoes*
         and reports target nearly stopped.

1957 - *S 3 ? miles from DofY - on fire*
         and damaged

2005 - *C in C to CS10. Can you now sink the*
                            target if I leave you
2103 - *C in C to Admy Scharnhorst sunk*

encounter of the battleship dinosaurs, took place this Boxing Day of 1943; henceforth wars at sea would be dominated by aircraft carriers and enormous nuclear submarines.

Admiral Bruce Fraser was single-mindedly dedicated to the Royal Navy; he went to sea as a midshipman in 1904 and spent as much 'sea-time' as any Admiral now serving in the Navy. A specialist in gunnery, he was a brilliant mathematician and had several accelerated promotions during his career. Although much of his service was in destroyers, a spell of service in GLORIOUS (one of the few purpose-built aircraft carriers) shortly before the outbreak of war persuaded him of the value of the Fleet Air Arm, at that time the Cinderella of the 'private' navies.

He was greatly respected and especially noted for his empathy with the lower deck sailor and his junior officers. He was a bon-viveur who entertained handsomely on board ship. When he was ennobled following this victory, in the mould and style of Nelson he chose the title 'Fraser of North Cape', but could not adopt it as it was part of a foreign country. It was not until after the War that King Haakon, when he was restored to his country, ceded the freehold of the North Cape of Norway to Lord Fraser so that he could assume the title.

Despite all the excitement and distraction of the battle going on to the south of us, we could not relax the defence of our convoy JW55A which was under constant threat of a pack of eight U-boats: we managed to keep these at bay and no ship was even damaged. From subsequent records it transpired that as soon as the SCHARNHORST was sunk the U-boats, known as the Eisenbart Group, diverted at full speed to the estimated position of the sinking in the forlorn hope of rescuing survivors. So, unbeknown to us, the pressure came off as we headed south-east to the Kola Inlet and Murmansk. We arrived on the 29th in daylight with the whole of the combined squadrons of Fraser and Burnett already oiled and heading for home. We declared 30th December as a substitute Christmas day and 'piped down' at 1030, visiting the CPOs' and ERAs' Messes (dangerous dens of 'uncut' rum) before a merry lunch, head down in the afternoon, and finally turning in at 2 am.

We turned for home on Hogmanay with Captain (D), 'Bes' McCoy, in charge of the escorts and a 'fast' convoy (10 knots!) of empty merchant ships, taking a northerly route into the 23 hour daily darkness which provided cover from enemy aircraft. This passage was marked buy a marvellous display of the Aurora Borealis – my diary was quite lyrical about it *"Incredible Aurora Borealis – waves of light in seemingly vertical pillars – like organ pipes moving to their own music"*. By 7th January we had turned south in a rising storm with the upper deck impassable unless we turned head on into the sea. The convoy was dropped off east of the Faroes that day and we made for Scapa at 23 knots to anchor in Gutter Sound on the 8th, hopefully to be left in peace for a few days and enjoy our mail from home. There was a pleasant surprise when Kenneth, now flotilla gunnery officer in UNDINE, the leader of the new 'U' Class of destroyers, came over for lunch and later we went ashore to the new Officers' Club for dinner.

Our short-lived period of peace and relaxation was shattered at 0800 the next day when we had to slip our cable in the darkness and a gale and, in company with ONSLAUGHT as senior officer, head off south to Invergordon for a 'combined operation' exercise in the Moray Firth. There was nearly a mutiny on board as the ships company, particularly the sailors living on the mess decks, hadn't had a chance to sort out their living quarters and dry out their clothes properly following our return from Russia. The atmosphere aboard ship could be sensed as 'bolshie' and I remonstrated with John Hodges. He was very concerned but we had to grin and bear it.

At Invergordon we embarked a General and Admiral Talbot together with their staffs and sailed up and down the Moray Firth, ostensibly backing up landing craft and helicopters. That evening the wardroom, apart from Paddy Satow being left aboard on watch, went ashore to the Officers' Club at Invergordon and disgraced ourselves with some excessive high spirits to vent our frustration. I remember a double base fiddle belonging to the band being squeezed through a small lavatory window from which it never recovered.

The Captain, who had remained on board with his 'oppo' from

ONSLAUGHT, had to take stick from the local Admiral for the behaviour of his officers and as a gesture he stopped our leave for a week!

Chapter XIV

COMMAND AND HMS FITZROY
THE FIFTH YEAR BEGINS
12th January – 19th September 1944

Being now into 1944 I had started my second five-year diary given me by Kirsteen. I noted in it my hope that I wouldn't need a third. It is perhaps a convenient moment to comment on the problems, apart from the enemy, which we had to endure and counter to maintain a destroyer as an efficient fighting ship.

The weather conditions in the North were unbelievably harsh and whilst the cold was hard to bear it was the wet and persistent dampness we found most unpleasant. In our cabins the officers were fortunate to have an electric fire to dry off their stockings and underwear, but the living conditions of the seamen on the mess decks were really unpleasant and unhealthy. The men blocked off the forced draft ventilation outlets to keep out the cold when off watch; the resultant fug and dampness only increased the incidence of foot rot particularly as some were inclined as they came off watch, tired and wet, to kick off their sea-boots and climb into hammocks with their trousers and stockings still wet. This was quite a common condition which the Petty Officers had to monitor as it lead to nasty amputations of toes and worse.

The short steep seas which came with the gales in the relatively shallow Barents Sea made for a very tiring and violent motion in a destroyer; what it must have been like in a corvette I hate to think. When ice formed on the deck equipment and upperworks the resultant topweight exacerbated the ship's motion even to the point of danger of capsizing. The sailors, huddled on watch at the guns, kept themselves active with chipping hammers to keep the ice at bay. The Barents Sea had relatively low salinity levels, fed by the melting ice and freshwater rivers; it was therefore more likely to freeze than the saltier Atlantic.

In winter the persistent darkness had a depressing effect on the normally cheerful outlook of the crew and it was difficult to maintain morale in these harsh conditions. Reading naval history had left one sorry for Nelson's sailors patrolling off the French and Spanish coasts for months on end and one marvelled at the hardships they endured. But I would have swapped a couple of weeks in the Barents Sea in winter for a month or two blockading Cadiz. Our mid-20th century sailor was as tough as his predecessors. In these circumstances one might have expected the officers to have recourse to a 'stiff one' now and again but in fact the reverse was the norm and seldom did one have an alcoholic drink at sea. In harbour it was different but looking back on the wild parties I recall, more were fuelled by high spirits than bottled ones.

During one very cold watch on our exposed bridge I had a bright idea. After some enquiries I learnt that the company who supplied the electrically warmed flying suits for our comrades-in-arms in the RAF was bizarrely named Frankenstein & Co of Manchester. I wrote to them and suggested there might be a market for the Navy in Arctic waters and if they sent me a suit I would try it out and report back. On our bridge there were a number of 16 volt electrical outlets for Aldis signalling lamps into which we could plug a trailing wire. The flying suit duly arrived and amid much hilarity I appeared on the bridge and connected up. It was a one-piece garment like a boiler suit and was really cosy, but unfortunately it had two drawbacks. First, it wasn't waterproof and being padded took a long time to dry out. Second, the trailing wire to the power socket was a nuisance and hazard to everyone on the bridge. So reluctantly I returned the flying suit to Frankenstein and thanked them for their co-operation.

We were back in Scapa by 12th January and wondered what would happen next. It turned out to be a quiet run down to Rosyth screening RODNEY in company with ONSLAUGHT, then back to base, followed a few days later by a similar sortie to meet DUKE OF YORK at the Firth of Forth and screen her to Scapa; all this in one gale after another. At the end of January we were to accompany KING GEORGE V (KGV) with other destroyers, including UNDINE with Kenneth aboard, for fleet exercises but a gale blew up again and the show happily was cancelled. I had given Kenneth my ciné camera to take photographs of ORWELL but this opportunity unfortunately had to be abandoned.

At the end of the month we were off at last to the Humber at 23 knots for a refit and went alongside William Wright Dock into the hands of Amos & Smith where we had been before; we were deammunitioned by 1600 enabling the first two watches to go off on leave by 1000 the next day: quick work. Kirsteen arrived in Hull by 1800 and we settled into the comfortable Station Hotel enabling her to meet John Hodges and my messmates, whom she had heard plenty about, and to entertain them to dinner in the evenings. One of these was Lt Rae Tribe RN, our extremely competent and charming Engineer Officer who of course was particularly involved organising the refit together with myself. After ORWELL he progressed in the Navy to retire as a Rear-Admiral.

In October of 1943 a significant Admiralty Fleet Order (AFO) was published which affected RNVR and RNR officers. This was the introduction of 'Fully Qualified Officer Status' to Lieutenants and above who had certain qualifications and experience in major war vessels[41]. The principal effect of this established our seniority to rank with that of the RN and recognised the steep learning curve and skills which many of us had acquired since 1939. My Captain, John Hodges, had recommended me for this qualification which in itself had tacit implications. When it was confirmed I changed my 'wavy' stripes for straight stripes à la RN with an 'R' in the loop.

As a comment on this change in ranking by the Admiralty, as far as I know there were no instances of the dramatic accelerated promotion in wartime which were possible in our sister Services (i.e. there were Wg Cdrs and Gp Capts in the RAF in their 20s, and a never-ending stream of 'the youngest Colonel in the British Army' at 25). I am not criticising the undoubted merit of these promotions but pointing out that seagoing officers in the Navy (both Regular and Reserve) were promoted strictly according to their seniority. Their capability was recognised by the increasing importance of the job to which they were

---

[41] A major war vessel was a corvette or larger.

appointed, but their rank never changed. There were exceptions to this general rule; in specialist branches of the RNVR, in shore-based jobs such as the Intelligence and Paymaster branches, and in the 'private' navies of the Coastal Forces. But as a rule there was no chance of a naval officer, however brilliant, either RN or RNVR, being promoted out of his current rank to become an Executive Officer such as a Commander on a cruiser or a Captain (D) before reaching the due date of his substantive rank.

On 23rd February whilst still in Hull supervising ORWELL's refit I had a letter from John Hodges, who was on leave, telling me my relief was coming on the 23rd and I was going to receive a command, at best a 'Hunt' Class destroyer but it could be one of the ancient and uncomfortable four funnel ex-American escorts. This really was a shock when the implications of the responsibilities attendant on such a position leapt at me. For over 4 years I had been an observer of the style and behaviour of many captains and how they handled their very isolated but complete authority on their ship.

Anyway it was a splendid opportunity for celebration and as Kirsteen was still in Hull we threw a party in the hotel before she went north the next day. I followed with all my gear when Scrym arrived back from leave and I had a moving send-off from the crew who lined the rails and cheered me on my way. I returned a couple of weeks later to formally hand over to my relief, Lt F R S King RN, and say goodbye to John Hodges. The train journey home was one of the worst ever; I stood in the lavatory of the train until 3.45am and finally reached Glasgow at 6.10am, being met by Kirsteen in a snowstorm. I went to bed for a sleep and then it was up and off in the afternoon to a Services International at Murrayfield with the Tindals, Willis Roxburgh and his father. Towards the end of February I ventured down to London to visit Cdr Deneys at the Admiralty and arranged some courses, particularly navigation, in anticipation of my new job, but mainly to chat him up to ensure a good command. Later that day I had lunch at The Ivy with Hamish Denny, our London agent.

The navigation course was at HMS DRYAD, the navigation school at that point housed in a lovely old mansion in Hampshire. There I met a number of old acquaintances such as Paddy Satow who was just completing his long specialist course, and Ian Morrison from Helensburgh, amongst others. In the middle of the course Kirsteen came south and we had a splendid weekend in London staying in the Park Lane Hotel and sharing a double suite (a sitting room and two bathrooms) with Willis. This all had the atmosphere of a French farce when the ancient waiter came in the mornings to lay breakfast for three in the sitting room for a chic blonde sitting between an RAF officer in a greatcoat and pyjamas and a naval officer in a Naval greatcoat and pyjamas.

After DRYAD I had a spell at HMS MERCURY, the Signal School, which was also based in a lovely mansion near Petersfield owned by Lady Peel. Here I joined up with a RN Sub-Lieutenants course. In the middle of this I had a quick weekend back home having somehow fixed a flight on a US 8th Army plane to Prestwick via Aldergrove outside Belfast!

On 3rd April I was promoted to Acting Lt Cdr with seniority of 31st March 1944 followed by confirmation of my appointment to HMS FITZROY, which for a while – and in something of a panic – I couldn't find out what class of ship she was. Eventually I discovered that she was a brand new American-built Destroyer Escort (DE) from the Brooklyn shipyard similar in tonnage and capability to our 'Hunts'. She was now on passage from Bermuda where she had been 'worked up' by her British crew before entering service here. The Admiralty re-designated these ships as 'Captain' Class frigates all named after famous Captains of the 18th and 19th century Navy. There were two types: the turbo-electric and diesel electric; FITZROY was turbo-electric, quieter and more flexible in response than the diesels. Her armament consisted of three 3-inch guns and eight 20mm Oerlikons as well as a 2-pounder (40mm) bow-chaser for anti-E-boat purpose. FITZROY was an inspiring happenstance insofar as it was the name of the young (23 year old) naval hydrographer Captain of the BEAGLE who in 1831 took Charles Darwin on his famous five year voyage of discoveries round South America and the Pacific prior to writing the 'Origin of the Species'.

I joined FITZROY at 0930 on 17th April at Chatham Dockyard and took over from the 'runner' captain, Lt Cdr Fanning DSC RN, the following day. I made my 'number' with the Admiral Superintendent Chatham Dockyard, Admiral Grace, who later came aboard to look around FITZROY. In many ways she was an advance on British destroyers particularly with regard to creature comforts: there were many more showers for the crew on the mess-decks and we even had a Coca Cola machine! I had an en-suite shower and loo as part of my spacious cabin under the bridge from which I had an almost all-round view – very useful. Goodbye to the 'folding lavatory' ubiquitous to HM ships large and small.

As we were to be in the dockyard for a few days Kirsteen jumped on a train and I met her at Euston and then on to the Sun Hotel at Chatham so she could see my new toy and celebrate my thirtieth birthday on 21st April before I sailed away again. As FITZROY was going to be attached to the 21st DF based at Sheerness I waited on Admiral Jack Tovey, CinC Nore, and had a pleasant talk with a man I greatly admired and respected. Kirsteen came aboard FITZROY in the afternoon but the next day, after going aboard in the morning for a meeting with my officers, we went off for the day to Canterbury and the cathedral, finishing up with a drinks party on board for the officers' wives.

On the 23rd we went into the sea lock at 1030 and I gave my first order *"slow ahead"* at 1100 before moving off down the river to a buoy at Sheerness. I had brought with me and was flying my uncle John McCulloch's commissioning pennant which he had kept from his ship in the Great War. It was a bit frail so after a few days I changed it for my own. Another formal visit was made on Capt Parry RN, D21, to finish off a special day. A couple of days were usefully spent exercising the armament and becoming familiar with handling the ship; fortunately the crew were already well trained from their work up period in Bermuda, but anti-E-boat tactics were practised as our convoy work would be in 'E-boat alley', the east coast route from Rosyth to the

Thames and beyond as the build up of materiel for the D-Day invasion began.

We joined our first 'FS'[42] convoy from the north at sunset on the 25th with the Senior Officer in the veteran destroyer WALLACE and had an uneventful passage south to Southend. Harwich gradually became one of our regular stop-over points for oiling and rendezvousing with convoys which more and more consisted of ungainly floating concrete piers destined for the Portsmouth and Southampton area prior to the eventual Channel crossing to establish what was to be the Mulberry Harbour on the Normandy beaches. Our speed of advance with these massive structures being towed by tugs was about 4 knots which with tidal streams of about the same rate made navigation extremely difficult. The south-going convoy we joined on 28th April consisted of three tows of concrete piers and some landing craft to be taken to Portsmouth. By the next day the convoy was spread over 15 miles reaching 20 by nightfall! Fortunately there was no sign of the enemy and the weather was marvellous compared to northern waters. The tugs involved in these tasks were smart new American vessels designed for this work, but they seemed to be manned by tractor drivers from the Mid-West. Having delivered our load we shepherded our six tugs back to the Thames at 10 knots and on 1st May were back on a buoy at Sheerness to enjoy a quiet day and catch up with our mail which included some delightful letters of good wishes from John Hodges and others.

The social life of the 21st DF started with a lunch party on the Hunt COTTESMORE where I met an old acquaintance from Clyde Division RNVR, Moray Murdoch, now Captain of VELOX, an old V&W Class converted to a Long Range Escort (LRE), and he was now a 2½[43] like myself. After another run north to pick up a southbound FS convoy, as an additional escort we went into Great Yarmouth for the day. This was an active MTB base for North Sea operations and I signalled a very old Clyde sailing friend, Walter 'Biscuits' Strang, to

---

[42] FS – Forth/South, FN – Forth/North convoys.
[43] Lt Cdr.

come off for lunch which he did by coming alongside in his MTB 668. We had a most enjoyable time 'swinging the lamp'.

This routine of shepherding (a descriptive analogy) the bizarre equipment for what was to become the Mulberry Harbours continued without much interference from the enemy; occasionally as we wandered through the Straits of Dover the enemy's big gun emplacements on Cap Gris Nez fired at our almost stationary targets but I never saw a hit registered. One of the most weird items we floated south, the subject of much speculation on our bridge, were enormous reels, like oversized electric cable drums nicknamed 'conundrums', which later we found were the carrying pipes for 'PLUTO'[44], the amazing pipeline laid under the Channel to supply fuel for our Armies when they landed in France. We parked all these various units at ports along the south coast from Selsey Bill to the Isle of Wight, returning north with the US tugs for another delivery from the construction sites on the Tyne and Wear[45]. When spending the night at anchor off Newhaven I invited a couple of USN tug captains aboard for drinks which was fun but confirmed my earlier comment about their provenance! As well as the special harbour equipment being escorted south there were convoys consisting of hundreds of landing craft of all types which needed protection; the build-up of the infrastructure to mount the invasions was quite spectacular.

Meanwhile I was uneasy at the quality of one or two of my officers, particularly my First Lieutenant whom I knew of old as a Clyde Division RNVR, so I upped my Divisions and mess deck rounds and in collaboration with Captain (D)'s staff stepped up practise exercises for all our armament and crew.

---

[44] Pipeline under the Ocean.

[45] The concrete caissons for the Mulberry harbour were flooded and sunk below sea level on arrival in their 'parking places' to remain out of sight of the enemy until they were required for the invasion. At that point they were pumped out and towed across the English Channel for the last part of the journey. The remnant of Mulberry can still be seen today on the invasion beaches.

Our radar equipment was rapidly improving as the war progressed, particularly the quality of PPI, with very clear revolving cursors, and of course FITZROY had the latest American-built sets. With the probability that our likely foe would be E-boats to be engaged in the dark in the waters in which we were then operating, new tactics were adopted and practised which required the CO to be stationed in the chart-room behind the bridge where the radar displays were fitted, with the First Lieutenant on the bridge conning the ship to the Captain's orders. The 'Headache' German speaking operators were also linked into this 'operations' room. So far, however, despite the amount of odd craft and equipment moving down the East Coast to the Channel, which German reconnaissance must have reported, there were no surface attacks on the convoys and this quiet time persisted until D-Day on 6th June.

Our routine until then had been the usual convoy protection and sheep-dog rounding up of stragglers in often foggy but calm conditions. There were not even U-boats in this area although the ASDIC operators were kept alert by the number of wrecks they identified in E-boat alley. Between convoys and patrols into the North Sea we began more frequently to use Harwich and by 25th May it had become our new base. We transferred to the 16th DF where Capt Salter RN was our Captain (D). This move indicated to me that FITZROY wasn't going to be in the first wave of the invasion force. Harwich was a pleasant enough base with an excellent Officers' Club in a large house called Michaelstow at Dovercourt, always swarming with Wrens. On board our respective ships, the Captains of the escorts entertained each other when in harbour and speculated on the outcome of the enormous gamble that was to come with the invasion of Europe. Some of us had been on the Dieppe Raid and witnessed the carnage there. During a stop-over at Immingham on the Humber on 27th May, I had three Captains on board for supper: Diggens of CURZON (a DE), Connell of COSBY (another DE), and the Marquis of Graham in LUDLOW (an old American 4-stacker) who was son and heir of the Duke of Montrose, one of the founders of the RNVR. I met him in later years when he was in Ian Smith's UDI[46] Government in Rhodesia.

After a much delayed southbound convoy due to fog, when we had to anchor all the ships in the night, we arrived in Sheerness on 31st May and met up with ORWELL and all my old chums who had come down from a boiler clean at Chatham. On 5th June I sailed independently from Harwich on patrol offshore in the North Sea to the noise all night and through the next day of bombers and air transports heading south. The balloon had gone up. At 0430 I anchored in Yarmouth Roads where we listened to the news on the BBC of the launch of Operation OVERLORD. Ironically our immediate commitment was the anti-climax of a boiler-clean at Chatham so I left the patrol area off the Norfolk coast and after a good trip up the Medway went into dock on 7th June. That night I was on a 1st Class sleeper to the north and was in St Andrews to join the family on holiday by 3 o'clock! Kirsteen had rented the Forgan's house at 9 The Links which overlooks the 18th green of the Old Course. Perfect! However it was a brief brush with bliss as on the 12th I was up and off early to Glasgow where I had breakfast with Dad and brother James, caught the 10am to London and was on board FITZROY at Chatham by 2230. I caught the first tide down the Medway, swung compasses at Sheerness and headed north to pick up a convoy going northwards. So far CUBITT was the only Captain Class frigate that had been called away from the 21st DF for OVERLORD. On 17th June however we took part, with eight other frigates and the River Class sloop SWALE as Senior Officer with Captain (D) aboard, in a series of exercises targeted at anticipated E-boat attacks.

At about this time Hitler's secret war-winning weapon, the V-1 pilotless plane or 'buzz-bomb', was beginning to make itself felt and in fact when I was on patrol off the coast on 19th June I saw a plane, apparently on fire, crossing to the southwards towards England. Thinking it was a damaged one of ours returning from a sortie to Holland, I decided to break wireless silence and sent a signal to alert our air-sea rescue services in case the plane ditched before reaching land. It was

---

[46] Unilateral Declaration of Independence.

of course one of the first V-1 rockets.

By and large life on the Harwich station was boring, consisting of patrols into the North Sea and convoy escort work up and down a featureless coast with no enemy to liven things up. There was plenty of social life, parties and even dances at the Michaelstow Club, and perhaps, as a result, a bit too much drinking. To counter this and activate sluggish livers I organised a rowing regatta (I had last participated in one with the 'Os' at Akuyeri) in whalers between the ships of the 21st and 16th DFs; training started with enthusiasm. Eight Captain Class ships were involved: FITZROY, BYRON, COSBY, DEANE, CONN, CRANSTON, and the sloop SWALE. The Admiral, Baillie-Groman, whom I had previously met at Devonport gave his support and on the chosen day, 12th July, all ships were unsurprisingly in harbour. There was great excitement and the contest went with a swing; seamen, petty officer and officer crews were cheered along the course on the River Orwell. CRANSTON won the overall prize. A week earlier I had telephoned Dad to ask him to donate a trophy for the regatta. He duly obliged and Baillie-Groman presented it. Stroking FITZROY's whaler, we won the officers' race by a length from CRANSTON. Kenneth, who was still 'G' of the 'Us' and was on his way south, had taken a side trip to Harwich to deliver the trophy and visit me, so as we were off on patrol that night he came to sea with me and the next day I dropped him off at Sheerness. He was on his way to join the 'Us' flotilla leader, GRENVILLE, in the Mediterranean where he took part in the landings on Sicily and Anzio.

The 'buzz bombs' gradually increased in number and gave us lots of target practise when on patrol but we never shot one down. The serious anti-aircraft batteries ringed around London, which was the enemy's main target, had little success in the beginning but eventually the situation was mastered with a quick supply of ammunition fitted with radar controlled proximity fuses. This effort was of course aided by the RAF who became adept at shooting the V-1s down in flight.

By 26th July we were due for another boiler clean so I popped FITZROY into Chatham Dockyard again and caught the night train to

Glasgow with Charles McNeill, my No 1, for company. The next day I was off to St Andrews where Kirsteen was finishing off her holiday at 2 Pilmour Place with the children and I was able to help her through to the West with them and the luggage. Good news came through that leave was extended for a few days which was always welcome. I took time in London on my way back to the ship on 5th August to visit Cdr Deneys at the Admiralty to ask him to replace my First Lieutenant and Sub Lt Morris RNVR. I recommended my No 2, Lt John Duggan RN, who had been promoted from the lower deck, to take over as No 1. When I finally returned to FITZROY there was a huge pile of orders dealing with the Normandy beached for me to absorb as, interestingly, that was to be our next activity. It meant a return to the 21st DF under command of Capt Parry. The first move was to sail over to Southend on the north bank of the Thames estuary for a conference with the captains of the merchant ships making up a convoy for France. I noted it was the August Bank Holiday so Southend was just the place to be!

I was Senior Officer of the convoy escorts and the first problem I had to deal with was thick fog in the Channel and having to anchor the ships in the Downs. By noon on 9th August we upped anchors and set off wearing tin hats on the bridge as we were moving under the falling residue of the anti-V-1 barrage from the guns on Beachy Head and along the coast. We arrived off the beaches at 1700 with the convoy safely delivered to discharge their cargoes and amidst an amazing collection of shipping, I anchored off Arromanches for the night. I hadn't time to go ashore on this trip but the scene through my glasses revealed, amidst shattered farms and villages, that the French had 'stooked' the harvest.

A few days later on the 15th I had another conference of merchant captains at Southend and in the evening again formed up for the passage to France. More fog delayed us, also causing a noisy collision between a merchant ship and a LST. We eventually reached the French coast in the middle of a mine-laying air raid by the Germans. Two human torpedoes infiltrated the anchorage that night and sank an LCT: one of the brave submariners was taken prisoner and the other was killed. The next day I went ashore to Courcelles for a look around the battered town. The Army had emptied it of camembert and cognac.

I sailed for the UK at 1100 on 18th August with our sister-ship RUTHERFORD and a convoy of 'empties' and at 0240 off Dungeness we had unidentified radar echoes at 2½ miles. The enemy had at last come out of its lair. I went into our latest anti-E-boat drill, taking up my position in the radar office, now re-christened the Action Information Office, with the 'Headache' boys passing me the translated orders being passed in German between three E-boats. Together with RUTHERFORD we illuminated them with starshell and opened fire with HE at which point they laid smoke and made off. Sadly they had made their mark before doing so, having torpedoed the leading ship of the convoy, the Liberty ship FORT GLOUCESTER. She managed to beach herself without casualties in the lee of Dungeness.

I was not at all happy with the way in which the new drill of directing and commanding from the radar office had worked, apart from the witless and confused performance of the First Lieutenant on the bridge. This arrangement was probably suitable for the patient stalking of U-boats and had been proved so by experience, but in confrontation with fast moving E-boats with the scene illuminated by starshell I would rather be on the bridge for instant and full control, getting the back-up information fed to me there. Discussing this dilemma with other convoy escort Captains and Captain (D) I found general support to abandon this arrangement and from then on when operating on the East Coast and the Channel, I was on the bridge. After personally reporting on the incident at a meeting with the CinC Nore, Admiral Jack Tovey, I phoned Cdr Deneys at the Admiralty and my First Lieutenant went to a shore job where he finished up the war with a brass hat. There was another unpleasant incident at this time; the CO of one of our 21st DF ships COSBY was dismissed his ship for smuggling.

Operation TIGER

Our general inability to counter the effectiveness of the E-boat was tragically demonstrated during the night of 27/28th April 1944, a couple of months before D-Day. In an operation called 'TIGER' raw American troops were practising landings, in anticipation of the invasion, on Slapton Sands which lie at the western end of Lyme Bay near Dartmouth (where I had my first encounter with E-boats on BROCKLESBY in 1942). The local population had been evacuated to give the Americans a free-hand to enable, apart from practising large scale landings, the live firing of artillery and rockets. It was just as well as due to a communications cock-up there were over 100 American soldiers killed in the preliminary exercises. At this stage the Germans obviously took great interest in what was going on and their daily reconnaissance aircraft, which had always been a regular feature over the Channel, must have reported the build-up of landing craft and troops.

The final exercise was to be staged over the night of 27/28th April to replicate the loading of the LSTs (the largest landing craft designed to carry tanks and other armoured vehicles together with all their troops) and their forthcoming passage across the Channel to the UTAH and OMAHA beaches on the Cotentin Peninsula south-east of Cherbourg. Accordingly the eight fully laden LSTs sailed at the appointed hour on the 27th to cruise round Lyme Bay for the estimated time it would take to cross the Channel on D-Day. Meanwhile CinC Plymouth, now Admiral Sir Geoffrey Layton, must have been aware of what was going on with these ships and troops in his command area but there appears to have been little co-operation between his staff and the American admiral and general in charge of 'TIGER'. It was of course the Royal Navy's responsibility to support such manoeuvres in the Channel. Did the Americans think they knew better than the Brits in not asking for or rejecting the support provided for every Channel convoy? In the event the E-boats of the Cherbourg flotilla were well briefed about this incredible target and were alerted by the increased radio traffic around Dartmouth on the 27th that the LSTs had sailed: maybe the Germans thought another Dieppe-type raid was being launched.

At 0200 on the morning of the 28th nine E-boats found the LSTs in Lyme Bay about 12 miles west of Portland Bill and had what the Americans would call a 'turkey-shoot'. The LSTs had only one corvette, the AZALEA, to escort them (a second escort had returned to Devonport with engine trouble) whose radio was not even tuned to the LSTs' wavelength. Unopposed, the E-boats torpedoed two LSTs, sinking one and badly damaging the other which limped back to Dartmouth. My old ship ORWELL together with OFFA now based at Devonport were belatedly despatched to intercept the E-boats returning to Cherbourg but the enemy made their escape unscathed. The casualties were hideous, with many of the troops sitting in their vehicles below decks being burnt to death. The death toll overall was about 800. Apart from the tragic deaths, the loss of three LSTs severely affected the D-day logistic plans – the loss of the tank carriers and tanks demonstrated how tight the margins were for mounting the invasion. The whole fiasco was rigorously hushed-up and reports of the action and losses were not published either in the UK or the USA until 50 years later. Rumours however quickly circulated, in the Navy at least and in FITZROY at the other end of the English Channel I heard of 'E-boats beating up an American amphibious training exercise'. My old ship ORWELL together with OFFA were belatedly dispatched from Plymouth to intercept the E-boats returning to Cherbourg but they made off unscathed.

Better liaison with the CinC's office in Devonport would have highlighted the presence and danger of the Cherbourg E-boats and a proper escort for the US LSTs provided. Experience might also have suggested the only way to prevent an attack on such an important target so close to a 40-knot torpedo-carrying enemy was to station a flotilla of MGBs off Cherbourg breakwater on the vital night. The Navy did neutralise the Cherbourg E-boats when OVERLORD was launched on 6th June.

Returning to my own story, the action off Dungeness on 18th August was the last time I confronted E-boats and I think it is fair comment that throughout the war they had the upper hand in most actions. This date also marked my five years at sea since the war started and I began to think I was settling down to it as a way of life!

There was evidence and intelligence coming through that U–boats were being deployed close inshore at both ends of the Channel to disrupt the flow of supplies to the beaches. After delivering a convoy to JUNO Beach I anchored nearby for the night of 20th August. On the way home the next day with some more 'empties' we had several contacts on the ASDIC and discouraged whoever it was by dropping depth-charges.

Another irritating device we had to be aware of was a clever mine laid in the shallow water along the landing beaches called by us an 'oyster' mine; it was activated at speeds over 7 knots. Although we did respect them and crept about when close inshore, I did manage to set one off which shook us up but fortunately caused no harm. The big guns on the French coast were very active at this time and together with the fallout from our own anti-aircraft guns engaging waves of 'buzz-bombs' heading for London, the passage through the straits of Dover was nerve-racking. In daylight we were often supported by a flotilla of MLs laying a smoke-screen to the south of the convoy to blank us off from the French coast and the guns.

I had a pleasant interlude on the 26th when I took the ship's motor-boat up the Medway from Sheerness to Chatham Dockyard where John Hodges was now serving as No 1 at the barracks and Nigel Pumphrey was visiting. I had a splendid dinner with lots of 'shop-talk' and gossip, returning late back to FITZROY at Sheerness before going over to Southend the next morning for another convoy conference then off to France.

To complete my officer complement a Sub Lt W A Morris RNVR was appointed who turned out to be very competent and an asset to the team. It is time I mentioned our Engineer Officer; Lt Bill Campbell RNR had been with the ship since she was building in the States. His pre-war job was as a manager with the Singapore Power Company until he escaped when Singapore was overrun by the Japanese. This background ideally qualified him to be in charge of the machinery of a turbo-electric driven ship whose controls in the engine room seemed to be one huge switchboard. Propulsion by these turbo-electric engines had one huge advantage in that they could go into reverse with speed and ease. Bill Campbell was a little older than me with a quiet manner and a good steadying influence in the Wardroom!

As we moved into September and the Army slowly fought its way across France, supported by the second phase of landings in the South of France, the convoys of supplies continued through the Straits of Dover and the Western Approaches and funnelled into the Mulberry harbour on the Cherbourg Peninsula. Quite often, and especially at night, we saw the gun flashes of our forces as they progressed eastwards along the French coast and a tangible sign of their advance was seeing a flotilla of our minesweepers on 6th September laying buoys for a channel into Dieppe. The big guns on Cap Gris Nez had not yet been overrun by the Army and were still firing at us as we sailed slowly through the straits. When we saw the flashes from the gun barrels we counted 60 and then ducked!

The 6th September also brought a great gale and I anchored the convoy and ourselves off Newhaven. By evening the gale was still increasing and our anchor cable parted losing the anchor, so we made for shelter in the lee of Eastbourne: but there it wasn't any better so it was now every man for himself and the escorts returned through the Straits and anchored in The Downs. Our gyro compass had also broken down which was most irritating. We were ordered up to Harwich where I heard that we were off to Belfast and on 7th September we sailed northabout in company with two other DEs, DEANE and REDMILL. It was a stormy passage in a north-westerly gale through the Pentland Firth at 0100 and The Minches at dawn just managing to maintain 20 knots in the conditions. The weather improved and was lovely as we sighted Inistrahull at 1500 and sailed into our new base in Belfast at 1930 on 10th September. We were there to operate against the latest inshore U-boat campaign which had developed around our shores. Many of the U-boats being deployed were now fitted with the snorkel device and used the 'Gnat' torpedoes that I mentioned earlier had been developed in 1943. They had already been active in the English Channel but without much success. The convoys to Russia were being mounted as before so the U-boat packs also remained active in the Barents Sea. I called on Captain (D) and his staff to be briefed and updated on the latest A/S techniques and enemy tactics and then made a courtesy call on FOIC, Rear Admiral Bevan.

Duggan, my new No 1, shopped around the base and managed to find a replacement anchor from another DE that had been 'Gnatted' by a U-boat. As usual we weren't allowed to relax for long being despatched at 2030 on the 12th to rendezvous with the battleship RODNEY off The Smalls at the mouth of the Bristol Channel and take over from SALADIN as Senior Officer escort together with DEANE and REDMILL. We turned north and passed through The Minches in the dark with bad visibility in driving rain – a very uncomfortable and worrying passage. However we left RODNEY safely at the Hoxa Gate to Scapa Flow and turned back for Belfast at 20 knots. There was fog that evening resulting in another trying all-night stand on the bridge as I led the little flotilla through The Minches. Fortunately buoys had been laid right through this long and twisting channel and, providing one didn't miss one on the radar, all was well.

Belfast was quite a pleasant base for the sailors to enjoy a run ashore and on one occasion we entertained the heavy-weight champion boxer, Jack Doyle, on board. He was a popular singer and gave us a sing-song on the foc'sle mess deck which was great fun, after which we retired to the wardroom for drinks. He was accompanied by a troupe of charming ladies of doubtful repute. The watering hole for the officers of the ships was the Ulster Yacht Club over which Lord Kilmoray seemed to preside and made us very welcome.

Chapter XV

AN INTERLUDE AT GREENWICH NAVAL COLLEGE
20ᵗʰ September 1944 – 23ʳᵈ February 1945

Following my recent visit to Cdr Deneys at the Admiralty I received a not unexpected personal signal on 18ᵗʰ September advising me that I had been appointed to the next Naval Staff Course at the Royal Naval College, Greenwich starting on 9ᵗʰ October, and that my relief was on his way. He turned out to be a Canadian, Lt Cdr O G Clarke, and I started handing over the confidential books and briefing him on the idiosyncrasies of FITZTROY and her officers. I arranged with Captain (D) to drive myself home so I left Belfast at 0930 on 20ᵗʰ September heading for the Clyde, not without an alarming incident as I turned the ship on leaving Bangor Bay. The anchor cable had 'come home' and I had rung down for revolutions for 15 knots while the Sub Lt on the foc'sle was supervising the securing of the cable with the 'slip shackle' when the opposite happened and the cable took charge and roared out the hawse pipe with clouds of rust and sparks. The foc'sle party leapt back as the power lashing around was lethal and they could do nothing to arrest the anchor and cable plunging to the bottom. I shouted down the voice pipe *"Stop both – full astern!"* at which point there was a wonderful demonstration of the flexibility of turbo-electric engines. In what seemed seconds as the anchor and lots of cable, but not as far as the clench, hit the bottom of the shallow bay, FITZROY came to a shuddering halt. We had saved the anchor and cable, and avoided much potential damage and injury. When all was safely on board and secured, I headed for Rothesay where I handed over to Clarke, and then crossed over to Wemyss Bay on the mainland where I was met by Dad and so to home. FITZROY was engaged for some time hunting the inshore waters for waiting U-boats and together with DEANE and REDMILL caught one near Islay. She also took part

Royal Naval Staff College, Greenwich Staff Course Autumn 1944
Back Row: Wg Cdr Radford DSO DFC AFC RAF, Lt Cdr Whalley RCNVR, Lt Briggs RNVR, Lt Caflat RNVR, Lt Cook RNVR, Lt Chesterman DSC† RNR, Lt Wade RNVR, Lt Cdr Crichton DSC RNVR.
Middle Row: Maj Dewar-Durie A and SH, Lt Webber RN, Lt Cdr Miller DSC RNVR, Capt Burton RM, Lt Cdr Baker RN, Lt Cdr Tresseter RN, Lt Cdr Meares DSC RN, Lt Cdr Wingfield DSO DSC RN, Lt Cdr Alleston RANVR, Lt Cdr Edwards RNVR, Lt Cdr Hewitt DSC† RN, Cdr Stovheill DSC† R Nor N
Front Row: 2nd Offr Ackery WRNS, Cdr Birch DSC RNR, Cdr(E) Taylor RN, Cdr(S) Colville DSC RN, Gp Capt Adnams RAF, Capt Addis DSO RN, Cdr Stitt RN, Cdr Wright DSC† RN, Lt Col Phillips RM, Cdr Longmuir DSC RNR, 2nd Offr Archer WRNS
Missing: Cdr Napier SANF, Lt Cdr Scotland RN, Lt Campbell RN

The author with his family
Kirsteen, Sue and Mike in 1944

RNVR Club (Scotland) Committee 1947
Back Row: W S Strang, W A P Jack, M Sandeman OBE, A N Morton, J M Matheson. *Front Row*: A J M Miller DSC, Samuel F Strang MBE, J A Montgomerie DSC. *Missing*: Cdr M Nairn VRD, W A Gladstone (Architect)

NAVAL MESSAGE.

(GV629) Wt. 16687/D7734. 500M 7/44. B.A S T.

For use in Cypher or Coding Office only.	*Full Dist* 4

Via Gib.

Originators Instructions: (Indication of Priority, AIDAC, NOTWT For Exercise).	INTERCEPT GROUP.

TO: *All British Men of War.*   FROM: *Dm y*

Splice the main brace.

081500B

Book or Table to be used for		Initials of Cypherer or Coder.	Time of Receipt in Cypher or Coding Office.	Date
Cyphering or Coding.	Recyphering or Recoding.			
2150	*P/L*	*1530*		*8/5/45*

Copy of the signal issued by the Admiralty to all British Men of War to **'Splice the main brace'** in celebration of the surrender of Germany, received on board HMS *Wolverine* on 8th May 1945 in a convoy to Russia.

After a happy spell of leave pushing the pram, with no immediate sea-time in prospect and some golf at Western Gailes with three other mariners also on leave, Norman Cadzow, Terry Easton and brother Kenneth, I made for London and Greenwich to start the Staff Course on 9th October. It really was a considerable privilege for an RNVR officer to be appointed to the College and I believe I was one of the first RNVRs to be so selected. It was a wartime course, shorter and more intense than the leisurely peacetime courses; accordingly we were worked hard with little time off and requiring lots of hard work over the weekends. The Director was Capt Addis, one of whose assistants, a Cdr Wright, I had met before. My fellow students were a mixed and interesting bunch including an iconoclastic submariner, Cdr Mervyn Wingfield DSO[47], whose sardonic wit enlivened the classes. It was his submarine STURGEON which had acted as a navigational beacon, positioned about 30 miles off St Nazaire, as a check on the naval forces heading for the attack on the dock gates on 28th March 1942. As usual on the course there was an RAF officer, Wg Cdr Radford, and a 'Pongo', Maj Dewar-Durie of the Argylls.

One of the abiding memories and pleasures of the Naval Staff Course was living in the beautiful buildings and surroundings of the College at Greenwich; we had all our meals in the magnificent Painted Hall served by smartly turned out stewards, even to the wearing of white gloves. The quality and variety of the lectures made us sit up and think about wider issues when for the last five years one had enough to do learning the complexities of seafaring on the naval coal-face. Politics were not a part of the course. Our syllabus covered all aspects of the naval scene including the workings of the Merchant Navy world wide, naval intelligence (but no mention as yet of Bletchley Park or Ultra), civil administration in the constraints of wartime, and so on. These subjects were delivered by the top men in these various fields. Our input was to produce innumerable essays headed 'Appreciation of the

---

[47] In later years he crewed for me when racing at Cowes.

Situation'. Early on Kenneth phoned from London to let me know he was reporting sick to Chatham Hospital where he was admitted on 13th October with pleurisy. I visited him there at the weekend and he was very unwell, taking several weeks to recover. For years after he was always susceptible to this infection.

London – the Big Smoke – was handy from Greenwich by tube and many of us who lived far away mispent our weekends there. On three occasions I did catch the 1pm from Euston, had a lovely 24 hours with Kirsteen and the sprogs, then back to the sleeper to arrive at Greenwich in time for the 9 o'clock start on Monday morning. Kirsteen was only once able to come south on 1st December for a week in London due to the lack of help at home and her father's illness needing her mother's attention. We packed the weekend with dinner and dancing at the Savoy where we had checked in on Friday evening; a play 'Banbury Nose' on Saturday followed by dinner at Hatchetts then the Cabaret Club; down to Greenwich College on Sunday for a look around and lunch, the London Philharmonic at the Albert Hall in the afternoon and supper with my cousins the Thornes at Millhill in the evening. On Monday I was back at the College leaving Kirsteen in town then joining her in the early evening for a Tommy Trinder show followed by more dinner and dancing to Carl Gibbons playing 'The Lady is a Tramp' at the Savoy. On Tuesday morning I poured Kirsteen into a taxi for Euston and crawled back to Greenwich to *work like hell to catch up with the weekend's fun and games'*. It was great to be young and to live every precious moment. The Thornes, Escott and Barbara, whom I mentioned earlier, with their children Roger, Jean (Laurie) and Freddie were very hospitable and I spent many pleasant times with them whilst I was at the Staff College. Laurie Carder married the brother of one of the Wren officers, Pat Carder, who made up our play group at the Michaelstow Club at Dovercourt. On the 13th I went up to fog-bound London on our 'half-day' to see Laurence Olivier who was magnificent in the film 'Henry V' – hence my apologia on the frontispiece of this oeuvre.

One horrific incident marked my time at Greenwich. On Saturday 18th November I had just had breakfast and was planning to head for London when an enormous explosion shook the whole College; this was a V-2 rocket, which unlike the V-1 'buzz-bombs', arrived without warning and had a huge explosive charge. It had struck a Woolworth's store adjacent to New Cross tube station which is near the College and being a Saturday morning the death roll and injuries were massive. A number of us from the College spent some hours helping the emergency services.

The course finished in mid-December. I had achieved a reasonable 'pass' to be marked by the letter *'psc'* in the Navy List. On my way north on 15th December I called at Queen Anne Mansions to enquire about my next appointment. Unfortunately my contact, and may I say my mentor, Cdr Deneys, had been moved on and I was in the hands of a stranger. I was happily left on leave during which we sold the Arnwood Drive house and bought 'Hillcrest' in Helensburgh on 12th January 1945. In mid-February my appointment came through as a Staff Officer (Operations) to the Senior Officer of the build-up group to Force 'W' heading for the Far East and the Japanese front. At this stage in the war it was a real shock to contemplate setting off again for the far East and I was appalled at the prospect. I went down to Greenock on 14 Feb to learn more about Force 'W' and its mission, wryly to learn that it was to be lead by Admiral B C S Martin, my former captain in DORSETSHIRE, with Capt Nigel Pumphrey as Chief of Staff! Our headquarters ship was the River Class sloop NITH already lying off the Tail of the Bank. I had an inoculation for Yellow Fever that day but in the evening I wrote to the Admiralty to seek another appointment in home waters. Without much hope of a stay of execution I started looking out and packing my tropical gear and on 20th February joined NITH sharing a cabin with two other officers – by now not my scene. As we weren't to sail for a few days I pushed off back home to Hillcrest from where I could see NITH if the QUEEN MARY did not obscure the view. We were on the point of sailing on 23rd February, Kirsteen's 25th birthday, when a signal came through from the Admiralty cancelling my appointment – what a wonderful birthday present. I never packed my gear so quickly and jumped ship just before she sailed.

A few days later displaying a false sense of grievance at being pushed around I called on the Admiralty in London and fixed myself a sea-going job. This turned out to be command of WOLVERINE, a V&W Class destroyer based on Gibraltar. In the interval before joining her, I spent a few days at the Western Approaches Tactical Unit (WATU) in Derby House, Liverpool to brush up my anti-U-boat drills. Capt Roberts was still in charge but the bright light of the visit was meeting Scrym Wedderburn, ex-ORWELL, who was also on the course.

Chapter XVI

HMS WOLVERINE: GIBRALTAR BASED
23rd March – 21st June 1945

I was now waiting for a sea transport berth to Gibraltar which conveniently turned out to be the troopship HIGHLAND CHIEFTAIN lying in Shieldhall Docks in Glasgow. After all the weeks at the Staff College and on leave, with the end of the war in sight, this parting from the family was about the worst.

We moved down the Clyde on 28th March and anchored at the Tail of the Bank. Unfortunately by this time in the war all troopships were 'dry' in contrast to my passage from Freetown to the UK in ORONTES in 1942. However by a happy circumstance my cabin mate was an acquaintance Ronald Teacher, maker of the well known whisky Highland Cream, heading for a corvette in Malta. Between us we coerced Lt Murray Brown, an officer who ran the Clyde degaussing service and whom we both knew, to obtain a couple of cases of the right stuff from the cellars of Ronald's house across the estuary at Rhu and smuggle them aboard. Travelling on the HIGHLAND CHIEFTAIN was an ENSA party on their way to Gibraltar, which included Nervo and Knox and a chorus troupe; this illicit supply of whisky ensured our cabin had a strong hand in Spades to take a few tricks in Hearts for our evening drinks parties.

We eventually sailed on 31st March in a large convoy in stormy weather. I noted in my diary that I had finished my fourth book since joining! We reached Gibraltar without incident on 7th April and I joined WOLVERINE lying in the 'Pens' to commence taking over the Confidential Books, etc from Lt Cdr Clegg RN – he was mad keen to get away as he had organised a seat on an RAF transport to the UK which was a much better option than hanging around The Rock awaiting a sea passage. So, I helped him on his way. He had handed over a well trained and happy ship that had been based on Gibraltar for some time so the ship's company were well 'run in' and knew the local form.

Our duties were mainly carrying out anti-U-boat sweeps in company with other destroyers of the flotilla – four Royal Navy and four US Navy destroyers. Captain (D) was Capt P N Walters RN and it was a nice surprise to find Mike Tufnell, my old captain on BROCKLESBY now fully recovered, was Staff Officer to Flag Officer Mediterranean Approaches (FOGMA), Admiral Crutchley VC.

It wasn't long before I was put to work early on the 9th, although I started off on the wrong foot by getting a wire around the propeller when leaving the oiler. This was soon cleared with no residual damage except to my, as yet untested, reputation with the ship's company. There was heavy weather in the Straits as, together with MALCOLM, we took station on the escort aircraft carrier PURSUER to screen her on her way to Freetown. It was going to be tight for bunker oil so early on the morning of 11th April when we were in sight of the Canary Islands to starboard I closed in carefully under the overhang of the PURSUER's flight-deck and picked up a buoyant oil hose which was hauled in over the foc'sle of WOLVERINE to top up our tanks. This was a tricky manoeuvre requiring accurate station keeping by both ships at 15 knots. Shortly afterwards we left PURSUER to go on her way and picked up the HIGHLAND CHIEFTAIN, who had been to Freetown, and the troopship BOISSEVAIN to escort back to Gib. Unlike days of old there were plenty of aircraft and even US blimps (airships) passing in the blue skies above us. On the 16th HIGHLAND CHIEFTAIN peeled off to go on to the UK whilst we took BOISSEVAIN into Gib.

The next few days in harbour gave me the opportunity to meet the local naval staff and other ships' captains as well as finding my way through the tunnel under the Rock to picnic and bathe at Sandy Bay on the Mediterranean side. One evening I went to the ENSA show put on by the cast who had come out with us on the HIGHLAND MONARCH. Cicely Courtnedge (who had flown out) was the principal star with Nervo and Knox and Hy Hazel, who made her name after the war in London pantomime.

Before I joined, Clegg and the WOLVERINE officers had

developed a rapport with the Army ashore and their officers regularly visited us for parties in our wardroom. One of these officers from the Sapper regiment was a Maj Bill McMillan, a surveyor from Glasgow whom I came to know well and who joined our family insulation company after the war. My own officers were a pleasant lot, headed by my No 1, an Australian RANVR, Lt C B Dillon, a lawyer from Sydney. He was perhaps the most untidy naval officer I ever served with; his cap over his red hair was always on the back of his head and about to fall off, his uniform was ever a baggy mess, but he was able and efficient; he became a learned judge back home where I visited him in later years. All the officers were RNVR except the Gunner (T), WO Penman who was RN.

We also had a good liaison with the four American destroyers who were with us in the 'Pens'; they were the USS LAUB, McLANAHAN and two others whose names I cannot recall. It was a mutually convenient arrangement as they came aboard us for drinks of an evening (their ships were 'dry') after which we went over to them for splendid 'eats' and the latest films from the USA. An aspect of the US Navy which I did not admire was the brutal manner in which their Military Police patrols dealt with their sailors who had one too many ashore and were swaying back to their ships. They laid about the poor chaps with their clubs until they were often knocked unconscious and bleeding, and then thrown aboard like so many carcasses. I compared this to the low key manner in which our Jolly Jacks, who had had too much Jungle Juice ashore, were supported over the gangway by their messmates and, with a nod from the Officer of the Watch, were taken below – if they were obstreperous they headed for the tiller flat to cool off – a civilised solution. Although there was no black-out in Gibraltar there was an eleven o'clock curfew for all servicemen which was a nuisance when a party ashore was in good song.

As usual when there was nothing immediate to keep us employed, Captain (D) and his staff organised exercises with other local destroyers including the Americans – these had there moments as our signal books were not entirely compatible. A typical day would take us to sea at

0630, turning east down along the African coast with a flotilla made up of MALCOLM, VENGEANCE, EGGESFORD (a torpedo carrying Hunt), LOWESTOFT (a sloop), and several corvettes to chase a tame submarine, fire at a drogue towed by a Swordfish, or carry out dummy torpedo attacks with EGGESFORD. On one occasion when recovering a dummy torpedo my whaler was holed and nearly sank with its crew on board. It was usually about midnight before we returned to harbour.

The Straits of Gibraltar were difficult waters in which to search and locate U-boats with ASDIC due to their sub-surface currents caused by the cold Atlantic waters constantly flowing into the Mediterranean to replace the evaporating warm waters there. Consequently U-boats could enter and leave the Med without much fear of detection if they chose to run deep when making the passage. We did our best to frustrate them.

An indication of the turn of events in the war was an order from the Admiralty on 1st May to conserve fuel. This was the first time since the war began that such a constraint ever concerned the navy at sea; we topped up our tanks wherever we were in the world although we were aware when sailing with the vulnerable tankers we escorted that there was a human price to pay for this freedom. A minor benefit to this reining in and a speed restriction of 15 knots on non-urgent passages was that the 'keep-fit' exercises were abandoned!

We now had little to do apart from the odd sortie to screen and escort, in company with MALCOLM, heavier units of the Fleet such as the increasing number of 'Woolworth' aircraft carriers similar to the PURSUER passing down the Spanish coast on their way to Gibraltar and on to the Far East. On 29th April we escorted the battleships ANSON and DUKE OF YORK, in company with the cruiser SUSSEX and the new destroyers BARFLEUR and TUSCAN, also going east. This was a fine sight in the sunshine of a breezy and rough day.

I had however one difficult duty foisted on me on 14th April and that was to provide and command a naval guard for the 'Ceremony of the Keys' held in the main square of Gibraltar. This regular ceremony was by tradition the responsibility of the senior officer afloat in the harbour and it fell on me with a detachment from WOLVERINE to mount this guard. We practised the drill on the quayside and on the day, with the help of the Royal Marine band, managed to keep in step (I think) and deliver the 'Keys' of the Rock safely to FOGMA who doubled as Governor of the Colony. We seemed to pass muster as afterwards I was invited to lunch at The Mount at which I wore my last stiff paper collar as invented by 'Johnnie' Gieves to substitute the laundered ones.

By 3rd May there were many indications of an early end to the war in Europe: Mussolini had been shot, the German Army in Italy had surrendered, and Rangoon liberated. Suddenly on 7th May there was a signal from the Admiralty that all U-boats had been ordered by Dönitz to surrender and give themselves up to the nearest Allied port. This was followed on the 8th by a marvellous signal timed 08/1500B *"All British Men of War – Splice the Mainbrace"*. I have kept my copy of this symbolic (and practical) gesture.

WOLVERINE was duty ship at immediate notice that day and in view of the expected surfacing of some surrendering U-boats I moved out into the Bay of Algeciras which also removed the temptation for the sailors to join in the wild celebrations ashore. This sounds a bit mean but there was always the possibility of an aggrieved U-boat captain making trouble. As it was I held a heartfelt Thanksgiving Service on the foc'sle in this beautiful and historic bay in the calm sunshine with the Rock in the background. It was an occasion when a return to normal life began to seem a possibility. It was 10th May before a couple of U-boats, U-451 and U-534, gave themselves up to Gibraltar.

There were lots of celebrations ashore and afloat. On 20th May there was a Victory Parade for 3000 officers and ratings led by Admiral Sir John Cunningham, CinC Mediterranean, followed in the evening by a splendid firework display against the dramatic background of the Rock. On 21st May I sailed in company with the Hunt AVONVALE for the UK leading the only two U-boats that had given themselves up in Gibraltar. I had lost my navigator, Bill Hogg, to U-451 where he was the 'prize captain' so I had to polish up my sextant to ensure I didn't miss the UK. AVONVALE was detached to Lisbon to pick up the crew of U-941 which had scuttled herself in the harbour - I never did understand how an Allied warship could interfere in Portugal, being a neutral country. The U-boats were duly delivered to Londonderry on 27th May where I received the news, welcomed by the troops, that we were getting leave in the UK after paying off the ship.

Gibraltar Chronicle, Monday May 21st 1945

STERN JUSTICE THE RULE

DETACHMENTS OF THE Royal Navy, the Royal Marines, the WRNS, and ships and establishments of Gibraltar Command paraded on the N.O.P. hockey ground, Gibraltar, yesterday for inspection by Admiral Sir John Cunningham, Commander-in-Chief of the Mediterranean.

More than 3,000 officers and ratings were on parade, and Sir John Cunningham was accompanied by Vice-Admiral Sir Victor Crutchley, V.C., Flag Officer Commanding Mediterranean Approaches.

Addressing the parade, Admiral Cunningham said he looked upon the Gibraltar naval forces as guarding the gateway to the Mediterranean. This had been done so efficiently that the invasion of North Africa and Italy and the ultimate defeat of Germany had been made possible.

He called for renewed efforts for the defeat of Japan and emphasised that defeated enemies must be treated with stern justice and never more than cold courtesy.

Sailors were well-known for their big hearts and their short memories, he added, and recalled the words of Admiral Beatty in November 1918: "Sailors must contract their hearts and lengthen their memories."

From Londonderry I took WOLVERINE south at 20 knots, deliberately breaking the speed limit, to dump our ammunition into a deep hole in the Channel off the French coast. There must now be tons and tons of brass and lead in that deep hole as old warships were paid off. On 29th May I laid up WOLVERINE in Devonport to de-store and we all went on leave; myself to spend my first leave in Hillcrest, our new home in Helensburgh.

A couple of weeks later I was back on board and having manoeuvred WOLVERINE stern first out of No 3 Basin set off, this time at 25 knots which loosened every rivet in the lightened ship, for Barrow-in-Furness where she was to be broken up. After a final inspection by SO Reserve Fleet I made the last signals to pay off

WOLVERINE which then headed for the scrap heap after a wonderful service in two wars. These First World War V&W destroyers were splendid sea-boats and serving in WOLVERINE in the blue and bright waters around Gibraltar was as good as it comes. The officers and myself had a farewell party in the gloomy local hotel in Barrow and dispersed the next day, 21st June. They were a good bunch and I wish that I could have served longer with them.

Chapter XVII

HMS HOLDERNESS: RETURN HOME
13ᵗʰ July – 11ᵗʰ September 1945

By 12ᵗʰ July 1945 I was off on the sleeper to London to join my next ship, HOLDERNESS, a Hunt Class destroyer, which was supposed to be at Harwich but when I reached there at 1230 on the 13ᵗʰ I found she was at Sheerness where eventually, after a hot and bad journey, I went aboard with my gear at 2130 and took over from Lt Cdr Philip Cole RN. To command a lovely Hunt Class destroyer was an ambition fulfilled but I wasn't given even a day to settle down before being sailed at 1530 on the 14ᵗʰ for a nerve-racking assignment. I hadn't even met my Captain (D), Capt Gronow-Davies RN of the 21ˢᵗ DF, who was in the Hunt GARTH. President Roosevelt had recently died to be succeeded by Vice-President Truman who was now on his way to the Potsdam Conference to confer with Churchill and Stalin. He had crossed the Atlantic in the battleship USS AUGUSTA accompanied by the USS PHILADELPHIA and these ships had been met off the Scillies by HMS BIRMINGHAM and six Fleet destroyers who started to escort them up the Channel. Off Ramsgate our little flotilla of Hunts consisting of GARTH, HOLDERNESS and HAMBLEDON took over from BIRMINGHAM and the Fleets and fell in ahead of the battleships to escort them up the River Scheldt to Antwerp. You can imagine how nervous I felt with a completely unknown company of officers and men. Fortunately I soon found that the key man, my Yeoman of Signals, was experienced and unflappable. Our first manoeuvre at a closing speed of 50 knots to replace BIRMINGHAM and the Fleet destroyers flanking the AUGUSTA was a seamless 180° turn which went off perfectly. Our Captain (D), Gronow-Davies, had been to Dartmouth where the cadets practised these moves in the motor pinnaces.

We then carried on up the Scheldt to Antwerp harbour where we handed over our charges. General Eisenhower and his staff were looking on from the quayside; we then turned together in the harbour, cleared lower deck and gave the President three cheers before returning to Sheerness quite elated but exhausted.

Daily Telegraph 16ᵗʰ July 1944

BRITISH ESCORTS SKILL

In our first glimpse of the American President thoughts of the important work he has come to accomplish were momentarily forgotten in the admiration aroused by the faultless incidental display by the Royal Navy. The Augusta had been first sighted off the Scillies. British destroyers which then picked her up completed their escort duties off Ramsgate. Next three destroyers of the Nore Command, the Garth, Hambledon and Holderness, took over. These vessels executed a neat parting manoeuvre that was expressive of naval skill. The flotilla under Garth suddenly shot upstream with her speckless light grey paintwork standing out strikingly in the brilliant sunshine. Then she turned and her companion craft followed with the swift perfection that is the product of strenuous war-time experience. All who watched on the quayside or afloat were thrilled by the precision of the movement.

SAILOR'S TRIBUTE

As the destroyers swept past the Augusta, and her United States cruiser escort, the Philadelphia, the British sailors gave three rousing cheers for President Truman. He must have been greatly impressed by the tribute as he sat on deck above a gun turret.

On one of our visits to Brunsbüttel on the Elbe at the western end of the Kiel Canal I collected, together with a couple of German prize merchant ships and some tugs, Hitler's yacht, the GRILLE, to convoy to Rosyth where I anchored her just to the east of the Forth Bridge. Eventually I believe she was renamed and sold to Saudi Arabian royalty.

I note in my diary for Sunday 5th August, when we were lying off dreary Sheerness with nothing to do, I signalled Captain (D) that I was going to sea with HOLDERNESS and also signalled my good friend Lt Cdr Duggie Williams RNR, lately of the Captain Class frigate CONN but now in command of the Hunt Class EGLINTON lying in Harwich, that I was coming up for lunch. We secured alongside EGLINTON at noon where all ranks were entertained and those who wanted a run ashore were given leave: a popular day out! Duggie Williams who had been in the Merchant Service with Cunard before the war had a brilliant career in the Navy and remained on after the war, eventually retiring and joining Shell Tankers. He was a perpetually cheerful individual and a great companion.[48]

The next few weeks were spent convoying merchant ships, may of them German prizes, to and from Continental ports such as Ostend, the Hook, Ijmuiden and Rotterdam through the swept minefield channels. It was a lovely August and when at Sheerness I put to good use the 14' dinghy carried by the Hunts, sailing over to Southend and down to the Thames boom. That evening we sailed for Rotterdam at 2030 escorting the troopship ULSTER MONARCH and the VIENNA. One trip took us north to Rosyth where I had Kirsteen, her sister Jocelyn and my father through from the West for lunch and then had a couple of days at home where we celebrated Michael's birthday on 9th August with an excellent party in glorious weather.

Kirsteen came through to Rosyth on 11th August where we stayed in the ghastly Officers' Club for a couple of days and I took her for her

---

[48] I include this little anecdote of a freebooter jaunt as by a strange coincidence I was turning over my diary for 5th August 1945 that same day in 1998 when 'Bungy' Williams' obituary appeared in The Times.

first ever sail in the ship's dinghy under the Forth Bridge (no road bridge as yet) and around the GRILLE. She also brought through our cocker spaniel, Roger, which I took on board with me. He settled down well but was in danger of being overfed by his chums on the mess-deck. On one occasion in Cuxhaven he slipped over the side and went AWOL in Germany. A general signal by NOIC CUXHAVEN requesting any sighting of a cocker spaniel, occasionally answering to the name of Roger, brought the wandering dog back to HOLDERNESS.

John Hodges, now a Captain and commanding the cadet training cruiser DIOMEDE, was in harbour and put on a splendid dance on board that evening for the cadets which was great fun for Kirsteen who hadn't had much such social life in the past few years. At lunch the next day I had my old friend from DUNERA days, now a Lt Cdr, Alan Wills on board together with Kirsteen and Robert Urie, now a Paymaster-Cdr RNVR. All this happened in the excitement of the imminent Peace negotiations which were confirmed on 15th August when Japan finally surrendered; by then I was on my way south down the East Coast to the Nore, spending most of the night on the bridge due to thick fog all the way. I had embarked my brother Jimmy at Rosyth for the trip south but it wasn't much fun for him!

Another run to Brunsbüttel was on 21st August where our wardroom lunched some officers of the 5th Inniskillin Dragoon Guards who later laid on jeeps to take us to Hamburg where that overworked word 'devastation' was a true description of the city. People were living in holes dug into the piles of rubble. During the bombing the city had been engulfed in the dreadful fire-storm phenomenon. The Army were using the Atlantic Hotel as a mess and quarters where I gave my farewell dinner to my messmates. This occasion had an amusing outcome. Towards the end of the excellent dinner when the huge dining room was thinning-out we started the popular acrobatic wardroom 'parlour' game of racing round the room without touching the deck. This dangerous game was first demonstrated to me by Cdr Michael Le Fanu (later Admiral) when he visited us on board WOLVERINE in Gibraltar. In the Atlantic Hotel dining room this caused disruption, competition from the Army and some damage. The next morning the Commanding Officer of HOLDERNESS received a signal from the Provost Marshall complaining of the behaviour of some of his officers and demanding they be censured. The Commanding Officer responded with an apology and promised that appropriate action would be taken and any costs met!

We had a couple more escorting trips between Rosyth or Sheerness and the Elbe with German ships and on 19th August I logged six years of active service in the Navy. It was a Sunday and by chance appropriately designated a day of National Thanksgiving.

My application for release from the Service under what was called 'Class B' regulations (i.e. compassionate, job prospects or any other grounds one could dream up plus length of service) I learnt was being considered. Sure enough it was soon confirmed and on our next visit to Rosyth on 7th September I unloaded my surplus gear for delivery home before sailing on the 9th for Sheerness, flat out at 28 knots, where I reached at 1200 on the 10th. My relief, Lt Cdr Smeeton, came aboard and I stepped ashore for the last time at 1600 on 11th September 1945.

The following day I visited the Admiralty and was formally demobbed, being given a voucher to present at Olympia and collect a civilian suit, shoes, socks and even a trilby hat. That night I caught the 2040 train from Euston and happily managed a sleeper for the journey home to Scotland and a new life.

No more was I required to make the sharp change from normality to constant awareness and a mantle of responsibility as one ordered *"Let go for'd – let go aft"* when the bow swung into the stream to meet the cruel sea and sky once again.

EPILOGUE

After the War I was closely involved in the formation of the RNVR Club (Scotland) and the transformation of the Clyde Division RNVR training ship HMS CARRICK previously based at Greenock as the Club premises to be berthed alongside Carlton Quay in the centre of Glasgow. As the Admiralty cannot transfer ships or property for no consideration, on a visit to London I called on their Lordships and bought CARRICK for the Club for one Scottish pound note laid on a desk. I wish I had kept the receipt. Following an appeal by the Duke of Montrose funds and gifts in kind from shipbuilders and firms involved in the marine industry, backed by an enthusiastic committee, the CARRICK became an attractive meeting place and memorial to wartime sailors. The Club was formally and graciously opened in 1950 by Princess Elizabeth.

In the years following World War II the RNVR (now called the RNR) Divisions around the country were co-ordinated as a minesweeping force and allocated an up-to-date fleet of single screw Motor Minesweepers (MMS). They were smart little ships capable of 15 knots.

Although I had moved south and lived in Surrey I remained attached to the Clyde Division RNR whose Commanding Officer was now Capt Charlie Dobson RNR who as a Midshipman had been one of the Clyde draft sent to Hong Kong in HMT DUNERA in August 1939. He had served in the destroyer THRACIAN, sunk by the Japanese, after which he was a prisoner in Hong Kong until the end of the war. In July 1958 I had a call from him to ask if I could help with a problem. The MMSs from the RNR Divisions were assembling in Portsmouth for a combined exercise and the Clyde Division had no one available at that moment qualified to command a 'major war vessel' and would I take HMS GRAHAM[49] from the Clyde to Portsmouth? I was delighted

---

[49] Graham is the family name of the Duke of Montrose, founder of the RNVR.

to respond, so brushing off my uniform I flew to Renfrew, joined GRAHAM at Greenock on a Saturday morning and sailed at noon. At steady revs for 15 knots on the diesels we had a lovely sail past Paddy's Milestone (Ailsa Craig), down the Irish Sea then a nostalgic passage reminiscent of the WP/PW convoys in BROCKLESBY along the Cornish Coast, round Lands End and up Channel to Portsmouth.

On the Sunday afternoon before entering Portsmouth I anchored off Seaview on the Isle of Wight and had my family, who were there on holiday, come aboard for tea and a look round the ship.

Further enjoyable post-war contact with the Navy was maintained through the Royal Naval Sailing Association whose burgee I flew in many offshore races including the Fastnet and Bermuda Races, as well as serving on the committee and as a Flag Officer. In 1990 Kirsteen and I finally returned once again to live in Scotland and settled in Crieff. From there I have enjoyed renewing my old contact with the RNVR Club, making a point of attending the Trafalgar Night Dinners for 'the Immortal Memory'.

BIBLIOGRAPHY

Atkin, Ronald, *Dieppe 1942 – The Jubilee Disaster* (Macmillan, London 1980)

Busch, Covette-Kapitan Fritz-Otto - *The Drama of the Scharnhorst* (Robert Hale Ltd, London 1956)

Chant-Sempill, Lt Col Stuart, OBE MC – *St Nazaire Commando* (John Murray, London 1985)

Dunn-Pattison, R P, *The History of the 91ˢᵗ Argyllshire Highlanders* (William Blackwood & Sons 1910)

Gordon-Cumming, Cdr HR, Turner, Maj LCF, and Betzler, Capt JE, *War in the Southern Oceans 1939-1945* (Oxford University Press, London 1961)

Gregson, Paddy – *Ten Degrees below Seaweed* (Merlin Books Ltd, Braunton, Devon 1993)

Jeffrey, Andrew – *Time of Crisis*

Kennedy, Lt Cdr Alexander, *'Hong Kong' Full Circle* (Harrison & Son, London 1970)

Ogden, Lt Cdr Michael, RN – *The Battle of the North Cape* (William Kimber, London 1962)

Peyton-Jones, Cdr Loftus, DSO MVO MBE DSC† RN – *Wartime Wanderings 1939-1945* (1993)

Roskill, Capt S W, *The War at Sea, Volume I The Defensive* (HMSO, London 1954)

Roskill, Capt S W, *The War at Sea, Volume II The Period of Balance* (HMSO, London 1956)

Ryder, Cdr R E D, VC RN – *The Attack on St Nazaire* (John Murray, London 1947)

Schofield, V Adm B B – *The Arctic Convoys* (Macdonald and James, London 1947)

Thompson, R W – *Dieppe at Dawn* (Hutchinson, London 1956)

Van der Vat, Dan – *The Atlantic Campaign* (Hodder and Stoughton, London 1988)

Woodman, Richard – *Arctic Convoys* (John Murray, London 1994)

OVER THE HORIZON